Essays on the Life and Work of Étienne Gilson

Christian Humanist and Global Peacemaker

Peter Anthony Achilles Redpath

En Route Books and Media, LLC
Saint Louis, MO

En Route Books and Media, LLC
5705 Rhodes Avenue St. Louis, MO 63109

Contact us at contact@enroutebooksandmedia.com

Cover Credit: Sebastian Mahfood

ISBN-13: 979-8-88870-260-4
Library of Congress Control Number: 2024949508

Table of Contents

Chapter 1

An Abbreviated Biography of Étienne Gilson's Intellectual Life 1884–1978

Born in Paris, France, on 13 June 1884, Étienne Henry Gilson was one of the leading Catholic intellectuals of the 20th century. While he was generally recognized to be one of the greatest historians of medieval philosophy of his time, Mortimer J. Adler considered him to be one of the few great philosophers of the age. Gilson's early religious education started at home under the long-distance supervision of Ursiline sister Mother Saint-Dieudonne. In 1890, he entered the Christian Brothers' run parish school of Ste-Clotilde where, among other things, he received educational grounding in Latin, catechism, and love of language. In 1895, Gilson left Ste-Clotilde to start seven years of education at the Catholic secondary school, Petit Séminaire de Notre-Dame-des-Champs. There he underwent rigorous training in classical ("humanistic") studies that included ancient Greek, Latin, Roman and French history, mathematics, physical science, liturgy, and music. Gilson left Notre-Dame-des-Champs in 1902 to attend a year of studies at the celebrated Lycée Henri IV. While there Professor Henri Dereux introduced Gilson to philosophy, and he attended Lucien Lévy-Bruhl's course on David Hume. Gilson graduated from Lycée Henri IV in 1903 with a bachelor's diploma and certification from the Faculty of Letters at the University of Paris that would permit him to continue his studies at the Sorbonne.

Between 1903 and 1904 Gilson completed his pre-university education by starting a year of military service. He spent most of this service in Normandy during which, beyond learning the art of soldiering, he read Léon Brunschvicg's *Introduction à la vie de l'esprit* and René Descartes's *Les meditations métphysiques* (*Meditations on First Philosophy*). Gilson enrolled in the Sorbonne in 1904 and completed his studies there in three years.

Especially memorable to Gilson during this time were a course on Descartes he took under Lévy-Bruhl and a set of lectures that Henri Bergson gave at the Collège de France. Lévy-Bruhl's course so strongly influenced Gilson that he decided to write his doctoral thesis on Descartes under Lévy-Bruhl's direction. Other major thinkers with whom Gilson studied during this time included Émile Durkheim and Victor Delbos.

After receiving his *agrégation* in philosophy in August 1907, in October 1907, Gilson was appointed a "provisional professor of philosophy" at the Lycée of Lalande in Bourg-en-Bresse, the first of several lycées at which he would teach. Having secured professional employment, on 10 February 1908 (in a civil ceremony) and 11 February 1908 (in the Church of Saint-Apais) in Melun, Gilson married his cousin Thérèse Ravisé.

In October 1908, the Minister of Public Instruction informed Gilson that he would be transferred to teach at the lycée in Rochefort-sur-Mur. After teaching there for two years, in July 1910, Gilson gained an appointment to teach philosophy at the Lycée

Descartes in Tours; in July 2011, he was transferred to the Lycée of Saint-Quentin.

During this time, on 27 June 1912, Thérèse gave birth to the Gilsons' first child, Jacqueline Marie Charlotte. In September 1912, Gilson transferred to teach philosophy at the Lycée of Angers. He also defended and published his two theses: *La liberté chez Descartes et la théologie* (Gilson's first major work) and *Index scolastico-cartésian* (an index of scholastic terms that Descartes had used). He also wrote a very significant article for the *Révue de métaphysique et de morale* entitled "L'innéisme cartésian et la théologie" in which, while studying Descartes's doctrine of innate ideas in light of the teaching of St. Thomas Aquinas, Gilson started to shift his intellectual interest away from Descartes and toward St. Thomas.

On 11 July 1913, Gilson signed an agreement to teach philosophy at the University of Lille from 01 October 1913 to 31 October 1914. Before his move to Lille, on 11 September 1913, his second daughter, Cécile was born. At Lille, among other things, he presented a public course he had titled "The System of Thomas Aquinas" that, surprisingly to Gilson, was generally well received. During this time Gilson also started to do research into the mysticism of St. Bonaventure and to defend his thesis on Descartes before the "Société Française de Philosophie."

Gilson's academic career was interrupted by the outbreak of World War I. On 02 August 1914, Sergeant Gilson reported to Lille, to the 43rd Infantry Division, 28th Company to instruct recruits. Gilson's military life initially took him to central France. When he reached Courtine around mid-October 1914, Gilson started to read volumes of the work of St. Bonaventure that he had brought with him. By mid-June Gilson found himself fighting Germans on the front at Verdun. By November, Gilson was moving back and forth between Verdun and Beaumark, where he was a machine-gun instructor.

At Beaumark, between two shifts served in the trenches, Gilson composed the first of many articles he would write on the fine arts, "Art et metaphysique," which was published in the *Revue de metaphysique ed de morale* in 1916. A major German offensive (that ended with Gilson being taken prisoner of war on 23 February and transferred to the prisoner-of-war camp in Mainz) interrupted his brief stint at writing.

After a short stay in Mainz, Gilson wound up for several months in Vöhrenbach in the Schwarzwald. From there, in August 1916, he moved to an officers' prison camp in Burg-bei-Magdeburg. While at this camp, Gilson studied Russian and other living languages and, with the help of local book dealers who did a thriving business with the prisoners, continued his studies in philosophy. He even managed to publish an article "Du fondement des jugements esthétiques" in the Parisian *Revue philosophique de la France et de l'étranger.*

In February 1918, Gilson moved to the prison camp in Strölen-Moohr, Kreis Sulingen, in lower Saxony. Conditions in this camp were much more severe than in Burg. Still, while there, Gilson managed to give lectures on Bergson to other prisoners, and also at Burg when he was periodically transferred there.

Shortly after the end of the War, Gilson resumed teaching at the University of Lille and reviewed books for the *Revue philosophique de la France et de l'étranger*. In 1919, he assumed the position of professor of the history of philosophy at the University of Strasbourg, which was becoming one of the best universities in France. In the same year, Gilson published the first of six editions of *Le thomisme,* entitled in complete form as: *Le thomisme: intro-duction au système de S. Thomas d'Aquin.* About this first edition, in 1960 Gilson said in *The Philosopher and Theology*: "The book deserves to survive in this first edition as a monument to the ignorance of its author."

In 1921, while still at Strausbourg, Gilson published his *Études de philosophie médiévale.* In the same year, he moved to Paris to become a member of the Faculty of Letters and informal historian of medieval Christian philosophy, director in medieval philosophies and theologies, at the Sorbonne. Shortly thereafter, he was appointed to the Section of Religious Sciences of the History of Doctrines at the *École Pratique des Hautes Études.*

Between 1921 and 1923, Gilson's international reputation started to increase and he acquired a large following of students and some future friends, such as Henri Gouhier. His work at the Sorbonne and the École heavily concentrated on St. Augustine, and his work at the Sorbonne also focused on study of St. Bonaventure. During the summer of 1922, Gilson became involved with a private relief program to help Russian and Ukranian famine victims. Upon his return Joseph Vrin publishers in Paris released the second, updated, edition of his *Le Thomisme.*

As Gilson's international reputation started to grow, increasingly he began to attend international philosophical congresses and accept visiting lectureships. At these conferences he became friends with international scholars like Alfred North Whitehead and Ralph

Barton Perry. In 1924, Gilson published his magisterial *La philosophie de saint Bonaventure* (Paris). He also wrote articles defending some of his theses and two critical essays, one about François Villon ("De la Bible à François Villon," summaries of which were published in *Annuaire de l'École Pratique des Hautes Études* [1923–1924]) and another on Rebelais and Rabelais scholar Abel Lefranc ("Rabelais franciscain," published in *Revue d'histoire franciscaine*). He followed this last article with his famous 1925 work René Descartes, *Discours de la méthode: texte et commentaire* (Paris).

Between 1924 and 1925, Gilson also offered a course on St. Thomas's moral teaching at the Sorbonne. This course became the foundation for his 1925 book on St. Thomas's moral thought, *St. Thomas D'Aquin* (reprinted by J.Vrin in 1930 and 1974 under the title *Saint Thomas D'Aquin moraliste*). During this same year, among other reasons, because of the influence on him of Bergson and Drukheim, Gilson started to do research and write papers on the thought of François-Pierre-Gonthier Maine de Biran (1766–1824).

By April 1926, his scholarly reputation within France and internationally having become well established, Gilson made his first visit to North America to participate in an international congress in Montreal, Canada, devoted to the topic "Education and Citizenship." While in Montreal he gave a public lecture at the Major Seminary of Saint-Sulpice, and initiated his program to study medieval thought and organize medieval studies. After returning to Europe, before the end of July, Gilson inaugurated a scholarly journal devoted to medieval thought and its history: *Archives d'histoire doctrinale et littériare du moyen âge.*

On 20 July 1926, Gilson left France to teach two courses and give thirty lectures at the University of Virginia on two topics: "The Development of Thought from the Twelfth to the Sixteenth Centuries" and "The Evolution of French Thought Since the Sixteenth Century." On 09 September, he traveled to Harvard to participate in the Sixth International Congress of Philosophy to present two papers: one in a general session devoted to the topic of philosophy's role in civilization's history that is important for understanding philosophy's nature; the other entitled, "L'études des philosophes arabes et son role dans l'interprétation de la scolastique."

While at Harvard Gilson stayed at the home of Ralph Barton Perry and, between September 1926 and January 1927, gave two courses: (1) "Descartes on French Philosophy" and (2) "Medieval Scholasticism," which he also gave at Radcliffe. During this time Harvard offered Gilson a full professorship. While Gilson respectfully refused this offer, he agreed to teach as a visiting professor during the fall semesters of 1927 and 1928. Also during 1926–1927, Gilson gave public lectures several cities in the United States and Canada.

The first talk in the United States was at the *Salon Français de Boston* on "Spiritual Movements in Contemporary French Literature." The second was a 22 November lecture on Jean-Jacques Rousseau at Cornell. The third, a 30 November 1926 talk at Wellesley College on "The Evolution and Meaning of Medieval Philosophy." Gilson repeated this lecture at Brown University. He followed this with lectures to: (1) the Philosophical Club at Harvard, on 08 December; (2) the Alliance Française de Boston (about Jean-Giradoux, the playwright) on 15 December; (3) Albertus Magnus College on free will in the teaching of St. Albert the Great on 09 January; (4) Wellesley, on contemporary French literature, on 11 January, 1927; and (5) the University of Illinois on medieval theories of knowledge (based upon a recently published articles in the Archives "Pourquois saint Thomas a critique saint Augustin"), 15, 16, and 17 January; (6) the University of Chicago, also on medieval theories of knowledge, on 20 January; (7) Columbia University (on French philosophy) early February; (8) Barnard College (on scholasticism), early February.

Gilson's 1927 Canadian lectures were to: (1) the Institut Scientifique Franco-Canadien in Salle Saint-Sulpice (inaugural lecture on "Saint Bernard, Founder of Medieval Monasticism"), on 22 January; (2) Le Cercle Universitaire, in Salle Saint-Sulpice, on 22 January about "Idealism in Contemporary Literature"; (3) an audience sponsored by the University of Montreal (on "The Theory of Knowledge According to St. Thomas"), again in Salle Saint-Sulpice, on 24, 25, and 28 January; (4) Institute Canadien at Laval University (on "Le thomisme"), on 26 January (5) McGill University (again on St. Bernard's mysticism), on 27 January; (6) the Dominicans and the Alliance Française, on 29 January; (7) St. Michael's College at the University of Toronto (repeating the three lectures on medieval theories of knowledge that he had given at the University of Illinois and participating in an evening discussion at the University of Toronto Philosophical Society).

On 05 February 1927, Gilson left New York City to return to Paris, where he spent the rest of the winter and spring devoted to teaching and studying the works of St. Augustine and John Duns Scotus, refining his third edition of Le thomisme (which appeared in February of that year), and disputing about the nature of aspects of St. Thomas's teaching. At its second annual meeting (29–30 April 1927) the Mediaeval Academy of America elected Gilson a corresponding fellow and, on 30 June, Oxford University conferred on him a Doctor of Letters, *honoris causa.*

On 15 September 1927, Gilson again left France to return for three months to Harvard. Shortly after arriving in Cambridge, Massachusetts, Gilson delivered a talk at Radcliffe, on 29 September, and another the next day, at Harvard, on a topic later published in the Harvard Alumni Bulletin as "The Ethics of Higher Studies." During this time, Gilson started to experience disgust at his inability precisely and clearly to explain the thought of St. Augustine. At the time, he quipped that something in Augustine "defies systematization."

Gilson spent 03–05 November in Toronto giving three lectures on Thursday and one on Friday related to St. Augustine's psychological thought, and participating informal discussions on Saturday about their proposed Institute of Mediaeval Studies at the University of Toronto. Gilson called three of his lectures, "The Nature of Sensations," "The Origin of Ideas," and "Memory and its Metaphysical Meaning." He devoted the fourth lecture, delivered to the Philosophical Society, to matters that arose from the Thursday lectures.

His conversation on Saturday focused on establishing a professional institute for all medieval studies, "a laboratory of the history of medieval civilization," complete with offices, classrooms, mandatory classes, and collaborative methodology that would emphasize primary sources. Gilson returned to Canada to deliver three lectures on St. Augustine (at McGill, the University of Montreal, and to the Dominicans) and give ten public appearances in Montreal between 01 and 03 December 1927.

After returning to Harvard from Montreal, on 05 December, Gilson went to a lecture and reception at the Alliance Française delivered by Paul Claudel. On 10 December, he returned to give a second lecture at Cornell. Before returning to France, he decided to accept the offer from St. Michael's College at the University of Toronto and not return to Harvard on a regular basis. On 14 March 1928, Gilson responded to a presentation by Léon Brunschvicg delivered before the Société Française de Philosophie entitled "La querelle d'athéisme." This debate helped convince Gilson that opposition to growing atheism made important his presence in France. To Gilson's delight, his third child, a son (Bernard) was born on the day after the debate.

During the rest of 1928, Gilson received many European, especially British, requests to deliver lectures and teach courses. The first came from the University of Aberdeen, Scotland, to deliver the famed Gifford Lectures on natural theology. He eventually delivered these in 1931 and 1932 under the title "Medieval Philosophy and Its Present Value." For publication this title was eventually changed to *The Spirit of Medieval Philosophy.*

Between 1928 and 1931, Gilson also lectured at (1) Cambridge University ("Middle Ages and the Renaissance"); (2) the University of London ("God in Descartes"); (3 and 4) the Universities of Leipsig and Marburg ("Cistercian Mysticism"); (5) the University College of Wales ("St. Bernard and the Love of God"); (6) Lady Margaret Hall, Oxford (inaugural address, P. M. Kinder Lectures).

Gilson's lectures at Leipsig and Marburg spurred him to write two articles for the newly founded journal, *L' européen*, entitled "Autour de Benda: la mare aux clercs" and "Vues prises de Marbourg." In the first article, like his friend and student Henri Gouhier, Gilson defended Julien Benda's criticism of modern scholars and intellectuals for losing sight of the philosopher's vocation to love and seek truth. In the second, Gilson criticized French intellectuals for abandoning the older French system of constructing and synthesizing in favor of the fetishistic positivist method of fact finding, of mistaking scientific positivism with unavoidable rational logic.

Shortly after his return to Harvard in the fall 1928, Gilson traveled to Toronto from 01–03 November to give four lectures and meet with Fr. Gerald B. Phelan to discuss further detail about the Institute and talk about the Louvain and neoscholasticism. Two of the lectures were historical and textual examinations of the teaching of Roger Bacon. The third was a talk given to the University of Toronto Philosophical Society about medieval realism. The fourth was a presentation to clergy on the theme "Early Christian Philosophers." Also in 1928, Gilson worked with Fr. Phelan to start to assemble a book collection for the Institute.

Gilson's return to France for the start of 1929 enabled him to witness publication of his book *Introduction à l'étude de saint Augustin*, which drew much criticism from Catholic and non-Catholic philosophers, among other reasons, for claiming Augustinianism to be a Christian philosophy.

Gilson left France in the summer of 1929 to establish the Institute of Mediaeval Studies (later to become the Pontifical Institute of Mediaeval Studies [PIMS]) at the University of Toronto. He arrived in Toronto on 29 September 1929 and attended a Mass the following day formally to open the Institute. His duties as the Institute's director included doing a lecture course and seminar each fall; personally directing the Institute's students in medieval history, law, vernacular literature, paleography, and liturgy; assembling its research faculty (his general plan for the Institute was that it be directed toward research, not toward granting degrees); and, if possible, arranging for pontifical status from the Vatican.

Gilson entitled his 1929 fall lecture course "The Thirteenth-Century Oxford School." In addition to his activities at Toronto that year, Gilson gave two readings, plus commentary, of Paul Claudel's poems for the *Institut Pédagogique* and a talk to the *Cercle Universitaire*. He followed these up with a talk in Quebec on "Le sentiment d'amour au moyen âge," three lectures (on Sts. Bernard, Francis, and Dominic) in Ottawa, and lectures at Cornell and the University of Illinois. Following publication of *Introduction à l'étude de saint Augustin*, Gilson accepted an invitation to participate in an "Augustine-Thomist Week" in Rome, 22–30 April 1930, to mark the fifteen hundredth anniversary of St. Augustine's death. Prior to going to Rome, he published in *Archives* an important paper entitled "Les sources gréco-arabes de l'augustinianisme avicennisant." In 1930, he also published "Études sur la role de la pensée médiévale dans la formation du système cartésien."

Gilson entitled his talk in Rome "L'idée de philosophie chez saint Augustin et chez saint Thomas d'Aquin." (published in 1930 in *Vie intellectuelle*). Because of family illness, he was unable personally to present the paper. Later that year, he published a second paper for Augustine celebrations in London entitled "The Future of Augustinian Metaphysics" (published also in 1930, in Bulloch's *A Monument to Saint Augustine*).

In 1928, in three lectures presented to the Institut des Hautes Études de Belgique, Gilson's Sorbonne colleague in philosophy's history, Émile Bréhier, argued that the term "Christian philosophy" did not properly apply to any movement of medieval thought. During the early 1930s, Gilson busied himself attempting to defend his expression "Christian philosophy" in reference to some parts of medieval thought. He thought that, in their study of classical philosophy, medieval Christian theologians had done more than append Greek philosophy to Christian beliefs: beyond form and content, they had created a Christian philosophy.

Around 1930, Dominican Fr. M. -V. Bernadot invited Gilson to publish articles in a newly established journal, *La vie intellectuelle* (formerly a journal called *Nouvelle religieuses*) that targeted a largely Catholic audience. Desiring at this time to reach a wider Catholic audience of intellectuals, Gilson published two articles in the Journal: (1) "L'idée de la philosophie chrétienne chez saint Augustin" (later to be published in the *Acta hebdomadae augustinianae-thomisticae*) and (2) "Le problème de la philosophie chrétienne" (later to appear as chapter 1 of *L'esprit de philosophie médiévale*). In 1931, he published an article in *Études de philosophie médiévale* entitled "La doctrine de la double vérité."

On 21 March 1931, an important debate on "The Notion of Christian Philosophy" occurred at a meeting of the *Société de Philosophie.* Gilson and Jacques Maritain argued for the notion. Bréhier and Brunschvicg argued against it. Other participants included Xavier Léon, Edouard Le Roy, and Raymond Lenoir. Maurice Blondel and Jacques Chevalier sent letters, but were not present. Regarding this event, Gilson's chief biographer, Laurence K. Shook, says: "Gilson was finding that philosophical systems meant less and less to him. Philosophers, on the other hand, such as Aristotle, Thomas, and Bergson, were coming to mean more and more. It was the act of philosophizing, Gilson was beginning to feel, that constituted true philosophy."

A month prior to this debate (16–20 February 1931), Gilson started his Gifford Lectures with a discussion of the nature of 'scholasticism.' He followed these with lectures on 29 May–02 June 1931; 08–12 February, 1932; and 30 May–03 June 1932. While Gilson was giving these lectures at the Protestant University of Aberdeen, Scotland, he realized that the notion of Christian philosophy had ramifications for Protestant thought. As a result, he started to delve into Protestant theology, including reading Martin Luther, Jean Cauvin (John Calvin), and the theologian Karl Barth.

In 1932, Gilson gave a course on Luther and Christian philosophy at the École Pratique des Hautes Études that included an enrollment of twenty Protestant theology students. In 1933, he lectured at the Protestant Faculty of Theology, Paris, on "The Nature of Theology or *Fides quaerens intellectum*" and included Calvinism as part of his talk. In 1934, Karl Barth answered these lectures in a talk to the same Faculty.

Also in 1932, Gilson received a Chair in the Collège de France, an appointment he considered to be of the highest order. To accept it, he resigned from the Sorbonne and the École Pratique des Hautes Études. When he gave his inaugural lecture on 05 April 1932 on "Le moyen âge et le naturalisme antique," Gilson started a new era in his life that would last until 1951 during which Paris and the Collège de France became the hub of his intellectual activity.

Between 1931 and 1969 Gilson offered the following among courses and lectures at the Institute: (1) "An Introduction to Christian Philosophy" (1931); (2)"Christian Moral Philosophy" (1932); (3) "The Social Function of Christian Philosophy" (co-taught with Gerald B. Phelan, 1933). "Epistemological Doctrines in the Thirteenth Century" (1934). (4) "The Philosophy of Duns Scotus" (1931); (5) "St. Bernard and Cistercian Mysticism" (1932); (6) "The Itinerarium mentis in Deum in St. Bonaventure" (1934); (7) "Duns Scotus" (1935); (8) "Intellect in the Work of Albert the Great" (1937); "Plotinus and Saint Augustine" (1938). (9) "Roman Classical Culture from Cicero to Erasmus" (1939); (10) "God and Greek Philosophy," "God and Christian Philosophy," "God and Modern Philosophy," "God and Contemporary Philosophy" (1940); (11) "Being and Essence" and "Texts Relating to the Distinction of Being and Essence in Medieval Philosophy" (1946); (12) "Early Anglo-Saxon Humanism" and "Prologue to the Opus Oxoniense of Duns Scotus" (1947); (13) "The Infinite Being According to Duns Scotus" and "Texts Relating to the Notion of Infinite Being" (1948).

(14) "Applications of *Esse* in St. Thomas" and "The Seventh Quodlibetal Question of Duns Scotus" (1949); (15) "History of Medieval Philosophy" and the "Confessions of St. Augustine" (1951); (16) "From Traditionalism to Thomism" and "Books 11 and 12 of the Confessions of St. Augustine" (1961); (17) "Prolegomena to the 'Prima Via'" (1963); (18) "The Spirit of Thomism" (1964); (19) "Renewal of Metaphysics" (1966); (21) "The Problem of the Non-Existence of God: The Difficulties of Atheism," "Is God Dead?", "The True Problem," "Is the Non-Existence of God Even Thinkable?" (1968); "Language is Metaphysical," "Words and Meanings," and "Poetry and Metaphysics" (1969); (22) "Finalism Revisited" consisting of four lectures: "The Case for Mechanical Causality," "The Case for the Mechanical Cause," "Finalism and Physical Probability," and "Evolution: Teleology and Theology" (1970); (23) "In Quest of Evolution" consisting of three lectures: "Darwin without Evolution, "Evolution without Darwin," and "From Malthus to the Twilight of Evolution" (1971).

Between 1932 and 1946, Gilson gave the following courses at the the Collège de France: (1) "L'esprit de la morale médiévale" (1932); (2) "L'école cistercienne et l'influence de St. Bernard" and "La doctrine de saint Anselme" (1933); (3) "L'idéal sociale du moyen âge" and "La métaphysique de Duns Scot" (1934); (4) "L'étude sur la psychologie d'Albert le Grand" and "Les theories de la connaissance au moyen âge" (1935); (5) "Les fondements du réalisme medieval" et "Les origins médiévales d'humanisme" (1936); (6) "L'idée d'humanité: recherché sur l'histoire d'un ideal medieval," and "Humanisme et philosophie de Jean de Salibury à Pétrarque," including the love story of Héoïse et Abélard (1937); (8) "Saint

Augustin et le néo-platonisme" and "Les grandes crises de la pensée médiévale" (1938); (9) "Quaestiones disputatae sur saint Thomas d'Aquin" (1941–1942); (10) "Albert le Grand" (1942–1943); (11) "Les sources latines du platonisme médiévale" with a concluding lecture on "Le christianisme et la tradition philosophique" (1943); (12) "La dialectique de l'être et de l'existence chez S. Augustin" (1945–1946).

On 21 November 1933, Gilson returned to Massachusetts to deliver an afternoon lecture at Harvard about "The Social Function of Theology" and an evening lecture at Wellesley. The next day he participated in a "Heidegger evening" at Harvard at which time he gave Ralph Barton Perry a tentative commitment to come to Harvard's August–September 1936 Tercentenary celebration and receive an honorary degree. A few days later, he received another invitation to stay at Harvard from October through December to give the William James Lectures.

Around mid-December, 1933, Gilson presented a series of three lectures on "Le société chrétienne universelle" at Salle Saint-Sulpice, Montreal. At this time, Gilson started to become convinced that, by decreeing faith and reason to be irreconcilable and by separating the political world into one empire directed by the pope and another by the prince, Latin Averroism had fractured the medieval Christian hope of a Christian social order rooted in moral law, justice, and charity.

In 1934, under the influence of Fr. Phelan and Basilian Fr. Henry Carr, Gilson went to Rome with them to hold meetings with the Sacred Congregation of Seminaries and Universities to discuss a charter for the Institute. After these meetings, in late March of the same year, Jacques Maritain accompanied Gilson to a private audience with Pope Pius XI. This meeting put the request for a charter firmly on the Congregation's agenda. After a provisional refusal in 1936, final approval came on 21 November 1939.

Beyond this, in 1934, Gilson published *La théologie mystique de saint Bernard.* Also in 1934, in preparing a policy statement for another journal, Sept, which his friend Fr. Bernadot had just established, to unify French Catholics and reverse the French republic's educational program of secularization, Gilson repeated this theme of overcoming the political divorce between faith and reason. This policy statement then served as background for a collection of articles entitled "Pour un ordre catholique" that he published in *Sept* related to education and political and social problems.

Gilson's first article in this collection, "En marge de Chamfort," attacked French intellectuals for having formed their own secular priesthood for controlling politics. His second article was a review of G. K. Chesterton's biography of St. Thomas Aquinas, *St. Thomas Aquinas: The Dumb Ox*" in which Gilson marveled at Chesterton's ability to penetrate into the essence of Thomas's thought. According to Shook, reading Chesterton caused Gilson to realize that, just as Chesterton had seen English Protestant historians writing history backwards, from the perspective of their understanding of the Reformation, "Gilson now saw French historians writing it from the vantage point of seventeenth-century rationalism."

At the same time Gilson was writing these articles for *Sept*, he started to compile papers on a second major theme on which he had been working since 1929: Thomist realism. In the early 1930s, Yves

R. Simon gathered these papers together and published them in his "Cours et documents de philosophie." Gilson would later publish the articles in two books that attacked the notion that someone could be a "critical realist" and simultaneously be a faithful student of St. Thomas: (1) *Le réalisme méthodique* (Paris, 1936) and (2) *Réalisme thomiste et critique de la connaissance.* In these books Gilson emphasized that the first principle of methodical realism is the same as the first principle of all human knowledge: an existing being, something that exists. Hence, Thomists deceive themselves when they think that a Kantian critique of knowledge or some sort of metaphysical reasoning must serve as a starting point of doing philosophy.

Gilson published his first paper in defense of realism as a philosophical method in 1930 in the Geyser Festschrift (in *Philosophia perennis*, Regensburg) under the title "Le réalisme méthodique."

Among other neo-Thomists, in 1931, in a paper published in the Dominican journal, *Revue des sciences philosophiques et théologique*, Fr. M. D. Roland-Gosselin reacted negatively to Gilson's article. In 1932, Gilson answered Roland-Gosselin in a lengthier and more detailed article in the same Revue. This article would become chapter 2 of Gilson's *Le réalisme méthodique.* Chapters 3, 4, and 5 of this same book consist respectively of these articles: "Autour de la philosophie chrétienne: la spécificté de l'ordre philosophique" (first published in *La vie intellectuelle*, 1931); "La méthode réaliste" (first published in *Revue de philosophie*, 1935); and "Vade-mecumdu debutant réaliste" (also first published in *Revue de philosophie*, 1935).

On 13 February 1935, Gilson went to London, England, to present a paper on "Saint Thomas Aquinas" to the British Academy (published in the same year in Proceedings). Shortly after this, France named him a "Chevalier de la Légion d'Honneur" and "Membre du Conseil Supérieur de la Recherche Scientifique." This second position required Gilson to participate in works of public foreign service in education, instruction, and external affairs. In 1935, this position committed Gilson to present three special series lectures to the: (1) Institut Français de Vienne, 13–17 May; (2) Faculté Catholique de Salzbourg, 17–21 May; and (3) Faculté des Lettres of the university in Rio de Janeiro, late July–19 September (a survey course of fourteen lectures on the history of French philosophy and two talks on "L'action catholique" and "L'ordre catholique").

After finishing his lectures in Rio de Janeiro, Gilson returned to Toronto in September 1935 to start regular classes. Just as his course lectures focused on Duns Scotus, so did his public lectures. In the early fall he gave two Ottawa lectures, and then five in Montreal (for a group of Capuchins of the Monastery of the Reparation and his annual lectures for the Institut Scientifique) showing the authenticity of Scotus' *Theoremata.* He later published these findings in two journal articles: (1) "Metaphysik und Theologie nach Duns Scotus," in *Franziskanische Studien* (1935) and (2) "Les seize premierstheoremata et la pensée de Duns Scot," in *Archives* (1938). After lecturing in Montreal, Gilson then gave talks at: (1) Assumption College, Windsor, Ontario, in October; (2) Notre Dame University, the Alliance Française in Washington, D.C. and New

York, and Smith College in Massachusetts in November. Gilson returned to France in December, 1935.

Gilson spent much of the spring and early summer of 1936 in France preparing his Harvard lectures. After arriving in Boston on 29 August, on 02 September he delivered a lecture on "Medieval Universalism and Its Present Value" in which he argued that: (1) four foundations of medieval universalism existed (rationalism, realism, personalism, and the philosophical quest for "truth universal in its own right"); and (2) modern man can only gain by emulating this approach and comprehending truths through some intellectual, personal, and universal knowledge.

On 02 October 1936, Gilson delivered the first of his William James lectures, which were first published in English in 1937 under the title *The Unity of Philosophical Experience.* During the fall of this year he returned to Toronto three times (10–14 October, 7–11 November, and 6–9 December) to lecture at the Institute and meet with students. During the second visit, Archbishop James Charles McGuigan presided at the Institute's inaugural and the Institute started to function under provisional Pontifical status awaiting Rome's final approval.

When Gilson returned to the Collège de France for the spring semester 1937, he started his course on medieval humanism with the famous love story of Peter Abelard and Heloise. Needless to say, this course was a hit with the students. So, too, were Gilson's 1937 fall Institute seminar on Albert the Great and his 1938 seminar on Plotinus and Augustine.

Shortly after his mother's death on 24 March 1937, Gilson delivered the Richard Lectures at the University of Virginia. In this series, he returned to the Latin Averroist problem of double truth that he had briefly examined in 1931. This series was published the next year under the title *Reason and Revelation in the Middle Ages*.

Shortly before the outbreak of World War II, Gilson wrote an article entitled "Erasme: citoyen du monde" in which he sought to assess the upcoming war from a humanist perspective. Of Gilson's humanism, Shook says, at heart, Gilson was an Erasmian humanist who "wanted to end all wars and to liberate men to work out their salvation in the context of personal freedom. He believed that this could be achieved through the kind of education that fostered the acquisition of moral virtue through the writings of Cicero and Seneca, and through the teachings of Christ."

Gilson was in France when Germany invaded Poland on 02 September 1939. Likely, under direction of the French government, he sailed for Canada in mid-September. After arriving in Quebec City on 22 September 1939, spending time with friends, engaging in war propaganda efforts on behalf of France, and traveling to Toronto, on 19 November 1939, Gilson lectured in Montreal on the "Société universelle," a topic he had prepared to deliver at St. Michael's College in Vermont. In December, he talked to Montreal's Institut Scientifique Franco-Canadien about "l"Europe et la paix." After giving other talks in Montreal between 23 and 25 January, he lectured at the College Saint-Alexandre d'Ironsides and in Ottawa at the Alliance Française.

According to Shook, during this period, Gilson's main motivation "was to drive home to his Institute students that in humanism lay the best antidote to the venom of war. For Gilson medieval universalism, or "true humanism" as Maritain called it, held the key to the ultimate health in the human condition." Because Gilson thought that, to be of use, students needed to analyze Christian humanism philosophically, he thought he had to present humanism within the context of the lives of men who lived it. Hence, in the fall, 1939, after publishing his monograph *Dante et la philosophie* (Paris), Gilson offered to his Toronto students a public course of twelve lectures on "Roman Classical Culture from Cicero to Erasmus" in which he led his students through the transmission of classical humanism to Christianity through a series of renaissances covering the eighth through the fifteenth centuries.

On 18 October 1939, while Gilson was in Vermont, the Vatican had granted his Toronto Institute a pontifical charter. Within a month Gilson traveled extensively.

On 11 November 1939, Gilson participated in the Catholic University of America's fiftieth anniversary celebration. On 15 November, he lectured on "Racine, tragédien de la fatalité." He later repeated this lecture in Montreal. After falling ill during late January 1940, Gilson lectured to his Toronto students on "God and Greek Philosophy," "God and Christian Philosophy," "God and Modern Philosophy," "God and Contemporary Philosophy."

Between 02 and 08 March 1940, Gilson expanded these talks into his Powell lectures at the University of Indiana (published by Yale University in 1941 under the title *God and Philosophy*). In these talks, instead of focusing on individual texts and persons, Gilson shifted his focus toward general themes and tried to develop the implications of St. Thomas' metaphysics of being relative to the whole problem of God's existence.

From Bloomington, Indiana, Gilson traveled to Massachusetts where he gave a talk about "La France et la guerre" to French-Americans in New Bedford, Worcester, Woonsocket, and Manchester.

Following these talks, on 11, 15, 22, and 23 March, Gilson lectured about "God and Philosophy" in Harvard's Emerson Hall. During these lectures Shook reports that a question asked by Professor Ernest Hocking about the existentialism of Gabriel Marcel caused Gilson to become aware of common ways of thinking he shared with Marcel. Gilson would later say that Marcel was "perhaps the most authentic philosopher of these times: whatever he says comes from his very depths." He would maintain "that Marcel's thought does not take philosophy for its object or even bear on philosophy, but is philosophy, and that Marcel cannot be "systematized, "summarized," or "answered" because he refuses "to falsify the real in order to create a system."

After returning to Montreal, Gilson gave six lectures in French about humanist tradition, based upon his fourteen lecture Toronto course on the same subject: (1) 26 March, "L'idéal du De oratore"; (2) 27 March, "La culture patrisitique latine"; (3) 28 March, "La culture patrisitique au moyen âge"; (4) 29 March, "La bataille des Sept Arts, XII–XIII"; (5) 01 April, "Le conflit de l'élquence et de la scolastique"; (6) 02 April, "Culture patristique et origine de la renaissance (Erasme)." During these lectures he presented a talk on radio station CKAC on "Le français et la philosophie."

On 03 April, Gilson went to New York to start his return trip to France, where he remained for the duration of World War II. Apart from twice attempting to get Gilson to collaborate with them, and having Nazi soldiers billeted in his Paris apartment and house in

Vermenton, Gilson says the Germans left him alone for the duration of the War.

Soon after his return to France, Gilson started to do an extensive, fourth, revised and enlarged edition of *Le Thomisme*. Soon after its publication in 1942, he started revising it again in light of his increased understanding of the *esse/essentia* distinction in St. Thomas.

In 1943, in light of criticisms that had been lodged against his first edition, Gilson published a second edition of *Introduction à l'etude de saint Augustin* and of *La philosophie de saint Bonaventure*. In 1944, he published a revised edition of his *La philosophie du moyen âge des origines patristiques à la fin du XIVesiècle*. The success of this volume caused it to be reprinted in 1945, 1947, and 1948.

Between 1942 and 1943 Gilson gave courses at the Collège de France on: (1) "Quaestiones disputatae sur saint Thomas d'Aquin" (1941–1942); (2) "Albert le Grand" (1942–1943); and (3) "Les sources latines du platonisme médiévale," with a concluding lecture on "Le christianisme et la tradition philosophique") (1943). Gilson later published this concluding lecture in the *Revue des Sciences Philosophiques et Théologiques* (1941) and *Cherchez Dieu* (1943). Shook maintains that Gilson's choice to publish this article in these two Catholic journals "served notice that Gilson's perspective was shifting from philosophy toward religion."

Gilson's life was entering a new, spiritual phase in which he started to become preoccupied with spiritual life. Evidence of this turn is his article "Sagesse et société" in which Gilson deals with wisdom as a gift of the Holy Spirit.

As World War II came to an end, Shook says that Gilson became increasingly devoted to realizing the possibility of that *ordre catholique* he had advocated in the 1930s. He was convinced that German Hitlerism, Russian Communism, Italian and Spanish Fascism and American Deweyism had stood in the way then: each of them had focused on the production of their own brand of citizen, and none of them had seen a pressing need for the teaching of moral and intellectual virtue. Now, real changes were finally possible. In 1945, to address these changes, Gilson wrote an article for *Le monde* entitled "Instruire ou éduquer?"in which he argued for the need to: (1) have greater concern for students as individuals, not prospective adherents to a political cause, and (2) familiarize students from infancy with moral virtues of the individual such as honor, duty, justice, and piety.

He quickly followed this article with four others that had the same keynote theme: "The first step of any totalitarian regime is to seize the schools in order to have exclusive monopoly over shaping tomorrow's citizens." In these articles, Gilson sought to focus educators' attention on inculcating personal virtue, not the power of movements. He entitled them: (1) "Hitler fera-t-il notre revolution?"; (2) "La circulaire 45 ou: comment l'on se propose de pervertir la vérité"; (3) "La revolution ou l'amitié redressera la Cite"; and (4) "La schisme national." He published the articles in Stanislas Fumet's religiously-oriented journal *Hebdomadaire du temps present.*

About a month after publishing these articles, Gilson published "Pour une education nationale" in *La vie intelletuelle.* He argued therein that free education must include religion. Apparently, before going to print, the Journal's editor sent the article to General Charles de Gaulle, who read it shortly thereafter. In another article published around this same time in *La croix*, entitled "La liberté de l'enseignement en Angleterre," Gilson expressed his admiration for the open British conformist and non-conformist educational policy in contrast to France's closed State-controlled one.

On 15 March 1945, he spoke before a packed meeting of "*La Jeunesse Intellectuelle*" in *La Grande Salle de la Mutualité*. As a result of these educational works, Gilson started to correspond with many of the leading intellectuals in post-liberation France and to become recognized as a spokesman for them. As a result, the French Ministry of Foreign Affairs selected him to join his friend Jacques Maritain as part of the French delegation the 1945 San Francisco meeting to plan the United Nations charter, which was signed on 26 June of that year.

After returning to Toronto for a few months in anticipation of teaching his fall courses there, the French Foreign Ministry informed him that the Ministry had named him to participate in the October and November 1945 London conference designed to create the constitution for what would later become UNESCO, the United Nations Educational, Scientific, and Cultural Organization. Gilson served on the committee that drafted UNESCO's constitution.

During his stay in London, Gilson wrote five articles about the conference that were published in *Le monde*. Several others appeared over the next several years. In them, among other things, Gilson expressed his disappointment about the limited roles intellectuals would actually have in UNESCO. He also later expressed disappointment about the behavior of intellectuals at UNESCO's first general conference in Paris in 1946. In a radio discussion in which he took part with several other conference participants after the meeting regarding the question "Can UNESCO Educate for World Understanding?," Gilson maintained that the world would not be ready for global understanding until university education became more international than it then was.

Despite Gilson's heavy political agenda during 1945, in that year he managed to publish three articles regarding the relation between the existentialism of St. Thomas and twentieth-century existentialism: (1) "Limites existentielles de la philosophie" (in *L'existence*); (2) "Pierre Lombard et les théologies de l'essence" (in *Revue du moyen âge latin*); and (3) "Le thomisme et les philosophies existentielles" (in *La vie intellectuelle*).

Gilson used the themes of these three articles for courses he would teach at the Institute and the Collège de France. He entitled his fall–spring 1945 course in France, "La dialectique de l'être et de l'existence chez S. Augustin." He called his spring 1946 lecture course at the Institute "Being and Essence" and his seminar course there "Texts Relating to the Distinction of Being and Essence in Medieval Philosophy."

Since Gilson had not lectured at PIMS for over five years, he cut short his course in France to go to Toronto in late February 1946. He then conducted abbreviated lectures in Canada from early March to early May. While in Canada, he became involved in a debate about whether Canadian literature was, properly speaking, French or Canadian. Gilson took the latter position in an article in *Le monde* ("L'arbre canadien") and a Canadian radio address ("La 852e emission de la Société du Bon Parler," later published in *La patrie* under the title "L'arbre canadien: le canadien, notre égal").

Gilson returned to France in May 1946 and, tired and wanting to stay with his family for some time, remained there until the following fall. On 24 October 1946, the Académie Française elected him a member. After this he spoke on 20 November about "Pétrarque et sa muse" while giving the "Philip Maurice Deneke Lecture" at Lady Margaret Hall, Oxford.

Next, on 21 and 22 November, he lectured the Faculty of Divinity of the University of London about "The Judgment of Existence and Its Relation to the Problem of God." He returned to London in January 1947 to give a radio lecture. In March, he gave talks in Liège and Brussels. In April, Gilson went to Rome to participate in meetings of the Pontifical Academy of Thomas Aquinas and an international meeting to establish *Pax Romana* as an international movement of intellectuals engaged in the service of God. At the Pontifical Academy he spoke on "The Knowledge of Being." At *Pax Romana* he talked about "Les intellectuals dans la chrétienté" (published in the same year in *Travaux et documents*).

While Gilson was engaged in these intellectual activities, he had also become involved in the anti-communist *Mouvement Républicaine Populaire* (MRP). Thinking that, as a politician, at the time he might be able to influence educational reform, Gilson accepted a two-year appointment as a senator on the *Conseil de la République*. Partly as a result of these new political activities, Paul Martin, Minister of Health and Welfare in Mackenzie King's Liberal government, invited Gilson to address a Young Liberals Conference at McMaster University, Hamilton, Ontario on the subject of democracy scheduled for the first week of September 1947. Gilson later repeated the talk, which he had entitled "The Philosophy of

Liberalism," to the Political Science Club at the University of Toronto. The journal *Canada Looks Ahead* later published the address under the title "The Task of the Democratic State."

In the talk, among other things, Gilson argued for the need for the modern state to condemn oppression of individual freedom and extend and guarantee personal freedom, including economic and social freedom, and personal property ownership, to everyone. While in Toronto for the fall, 1947, Gilson busied himself with new courses on Duns Scotus and public lectures. In the spring, 08 April 1948, Gilson addressed the *Semaines des Intellectuals Catholiques* on the theme "Intellectuals and Peace." This lecture considered the post-World War II "Terrors" that would result from the West embracing Friedrich Nietzsche's proclamation of God's death. The lecture was subsequently published in 1949 in English, in Toronto, under the title *The Terrors of the Year 2000*, and in French under the same title, *Les terreurs de l'an deux mille* (in *La revue* and in *Revue de l'Université d'Ottawa*).

Early in May, 1948, Gilson participated in a meeting of the Congress of Europe in The Hague to discuss plans for a united Europe. Gilson published an article about the meeting in the paper *Une semaine dans le monde* and in an unpublished typescript that he wrote in 1950 entitled "Existe-t-il une culture éuropéenne?" On 10 May 1948, he spoke at the Cité-Club in Paris of the need for religious freedom in education as essential to the existence of intellectual freedom. Subsequently, he became involved in a debate related to public or private rights to inherit literary property. Gilson argued for the former in two articles entitled "Le domaine public" and "Les héritiers du roi Salomon" (published in *Le monde*). From 13 August to 18 September 1948, Gilson published articles in *Le monde* expressing his disappointment with professional politics. In December 1948, Gilson's professional political career ended with his realization "that there is no difference between being a senator and being nothing."

While Gilson spent much of 1948 involved with political issues, during this time he also did some of his best metaphysical work. He published his book *L'être et l'essence* dealing with the rise and fall of metaphysics and his hope for its revival. An English version of this work appeared in 1949 under the title *Being and Some Philosophers.* According to Shook, Gilson later considered this book "his finest work." Chenu, however, called Gilson's *The Spirit of Medieval Philosophy* "le plus beau." And, "although Gilson continued to argue often that he was 'only an historian,' he realized that with *Being and Some Philosophers* he was writing as a philosopher and putting forward his own kind of existentialism."

Also in 1948, Gilson published in the journal *Medieval Studies* an article that would become the first chapter of his book on John Duns Scotus: "L'objet de la metaphysique selon Duns Scot."

Shortly after Gilson returned to Canada in September 1949, he delivered an evening lecture at St. Thomas More College of Saskatoon on "St. Thomas More and the Law." He followed this with a lecture the next morning at the University of Saskatchewan on "Politics and Philosophy." In the article, Gilson argued about the relationship among tolerance, dogmatism, skepticism, and truth. He maintained that no necessary connection exists between dogmatism and intolerance or skepticism and tolerance. He claimed that skeptics qua skeptics cannot be tolerant and dogmatists qua dogmatists need not be intolerant. Skeptics qua skeptics can only be permissive, not tolerant. Strictly speaking, only the person who admits the existence of truth can be tolerant. Gilson argued further that tolerance is a moral, not an intellectual, virtue rooted in the political virtues of justice and friendship; and that tolerance and intolerance exist essentially in the political, not the intellectual, order. This lecture was subsequently published in the University's journal *Le Sheaf*. Gilson expanded the lecture, presented it at Rutgers University, and later published it under the title "Dogmatism and Tolerance."

In the fall, 1949, Gilson's courses at the Institute were scheduled to be "Applications of *Esse*" in St. Thomas and "The Seventh Quodlibetal Question of Duns Scotus." Shortly after arriving in Toronto from Saskatoon, Gilson had return early to to France. Word had come to him that his wife Thérèse was seriously ill. He returned to Paris where his wife died on 12 November 1949. Shook maintains that, after his wife's death, Gilson sank into serious depression that distraction from work on Duns Scotus and his course at the Collège de France, which started in December, helped somewhat to alleviate.

Early in January, 1950, Gilson presented a currently unpublished address to the MRP in Paris about "Political Liberty and the Parties." In the talk Gilson praised the movement's respect for the individual freedom of its deputies to be able to think for themselves, not tow the party line. He claimed that the party's program: (1) regarded the family, not the political party, as the real center of French social organization; (2) would not nationalize industry unless needed for normal production and distribution; (3) would support revolutionary union objectives only if they were legitimate; (4) would treat every French citizen as an individual moral agent possessed of intellect, will, and the faculty of free choice—not as a number; and (5) advocated no State religion, official science or philosophy, and did not discriminate in the area of teaching.

At this time Gilson regularly wrote political articles for *Le monde*. In one, "1940 to 1950," he described monarchists as "historical paleontologists" and accused Charles Maurras of being a "collaborator." He was, also, regularly critical of claims made by US politicians because, apparently, he thought that American foreign policy was largely based upon self-interest and that European politicians who reached out for US support also tended to do so out of self-interest. He thought that France's best interest at the time lay in neutrality between the Russia and the USA. He wrote three articles in *Le Monde* advocating European neutrality in case of war between the US and Russia: (1) "Défaitisme et neutralité," (2) "La neutralité vers l'est," and (3) "La neutralité vers l'ouest." At the time, to Gilson's amazement, some people accused him of being a "crypto-Communist" and "anti-American."

During the spring and summer 1950, Gilson prepared papers for two important congresses to be held in Rome during September: (1) "Congressus scholasticus internationalis" and (2) "Congressus Thomisticus internationalis." At the first conference, Gilson spoke twice to attendees, and once to a private audience of Franciscan professors about: (1) "Duns Scotus in Light of Critical History," (2) "Critical-Historical Research and the Future of Scholasticism" (later published in 1951 *The Modern Schoolman* under the title "Historical Research and the Future of Scholasticism" and in *Acta Congressus*

Scholastici Internationalis Romae Sancto MCML Celebrati), and (3) "The Prologues of the Opus Oxoniense." At the second meeting he spoke about "La prevue du *De ente et essentia*" (later published in 1950 in the *Acta*, *Doctor Communis*).

Gilson considered his paper on the "Critical-Historical Research and the Future of Scholasticism" to be "an H-bomb" because, in it, he had argued that scholasticism is no philosophy in its own right, that it must return to theology to function correctly. He claimed that medieval scholasticism had developed as a result of theology turning the light of revelation upon the metaphysics of the ancient philosophers, that it was a handmaid to theology, and that theology must continue to reflect upon science, whether the "science" be "science" in the modern sense or classical metaphysics.

After his course at the Collège de France ended in March 1950, Gilson went to Sweden, where, between 12 March and 02 April, he delivered eight lectures on St. Augustine. After the two congresses finished, in September, 1950, Gilson went to Toronto to deliver two courses: (1) "Intellect and Will" and (2) "Illumination in Duns Scotus." As part of his commitments outside PIMS, he agreed to lecture at: (1) the University of British Columbia, (2) the University of Notre Dame, and (3) Marquette University.

Gilson gave four lectures at Vancouver. He entitled his major address, on 16 November, 1950, "The Place of Medieval Studies Within the History of Western Civilization." The afternoon and evening after this talk Gilson met with students to discuss whether non-secterianism really protects academic freedom. Between 30 November and 02 December, Gilson presented four more lectures, at the University of Notre Dame, in which he more or less repeated the talks he had given in Rome at the "*Congressus scholasticus internationalis*" in September. He entitled three of these talks "The Fundamental Positions of Duns Scotus in Light of the Historical Research." He called the fourth, "Historical Research and the Future of Scholasticism."

At an after-dinner party the evening he delivered this last talk, Shook reports that Gilson happened to speak about the dangers he thought "an unarmed, partisan France faced from Russia." On Sunday, 03 December, Gilson repeated at Marquette the fourth lecture he had given at Notre Dame. After returning to Toronto on Monday, 04 December, on 12 December, Gilson wrote the French Ministry of Public Instruction that he wanted to retire from his position at the Collège de France starting 01 January 1951, something that he was legally entitled to do. He had wanted to divide his time almost equally between France and North America and to devote the next three years to teaching at the Toronto Institute to which he had given birth and had started to see grow.

To Gilson's shock, three days later, on 12 December 1950, *The Commonweal* magazine published a misleading, misrepresentative, attack letter by Waldemar Gurian (then professor of political philosophy at Notre Dame, head of Notre Dame's "Committee on International Relations," and editor of the *Review of Politics*) against Gilson entitled "Europe and the United States." In that letter, among other things, Gurian (an émigré from Russian communism and Nazi Germany, who did not attend the after-dinner party at Notre Dame on 02 December) unjustly maligned Gilson for: (1) using his time at Notre Dame to spread "the Gospel of defeatism"; (2) calling a respected French journalist "a paid American agent"; (3) choosing never to return to France and "the haven of the New World to a threatened Europe"; (4) trying to speak on international issues as if he were a statesman; and (5) helping the cause of world communism by undermining the "will to resist."

For a couple of weeks after the event, Gilson had attempted to get *The Commonweal* editor to print a retraction of the letter. The editor refused and, for several weeks, as several French papers and journals publicized "L'affaire Gilson" and falsely accused him of things like being a traitor, Gilson remained silent. During this time, on 11 February 1951, to its shame and discredit, the Collège de France decided not to grant Gilson an honorariat. (Finally overcoming some of its shame, on 05 February 1957, the Collège named Gilson *professeur honoraire*.)

On 17 and 22 February, Gilson finally broke his silence, publishing replies to his accusers in Paris's two leading newspapers: *Figaro littéraire* and *Le monde*. Gilson did not think his letter to the former publication had achieved much; but he thought he fared better in the latter in which he accused French Catholics of playing into Russia's hands by equating all communists with Moscow imperialists, thereby driving into Moscow's camp many people who were simply searching for different forms of liberty.

Gilson was living in Toronto when the "L'affaire Gilson" was in full force in Paris. On 22 April 1951, he gave a centennial lecture at St. Francis University in Antigonish, Canada. In May, he returned to Paris. On 20 June, Gilson received an honorary doctorate from the University of Glasgow, which was celebrating its five hundred year anniversary. On 26 July, Gilson returned to Toronto to deliver a lecture course on the "History of Medieval Philosophy" and a seminar class on the "Confessions of St. Augustine." During this year Gilson also published a work on aesthetics entitled *L'école des muses* (later translated into English by Maisie Ward and published in 1953 under the title *Choir of Muses*).

After 1951 until 1957, when Canadian income tax laws became too prohibitive for Gilson to work there, Gilson would spend seven months in Canada and five in France. After that, until he left Canada entirely, he would spend three months in Canada and the rest in France. 1952 was a busy year for Gilson during which he lectured extensively on three main themes: (1) ethics and education, (2) contemporary science and philosophy, and (3) Christendom as the City of God.

He gave his first talk on 02 February, Candlemas Day, to St. Michael's College Adult Education Program on "The Breakdown of Morals and Christian Education." He later repeated this talk, which was published twice, at St. John Fisher College, Rochester, New York, and other places.

On 22 February, he spoke before the Alliance Française in Toronto. Between 27 and 31 March, he gave three talks at the University of Montreal and one for the Institut Franco-Canadien (also in Montreal). In mid-April, he read a paper on "Science, Philosophy, and Religious Wisdom" at the annual meeting of the American Catholic Philosophical Association (ACPA), published the same year in the Association's *Proceedings*, on the occasion of receiving the Association's *Cardinal Spellman Aquinas Medal*. Also in April, he delivered a radio version of this paper entitled "Religious Wisdom and Scientific Knowledge." On 23 April, Gilson flew to Belgium to: (1) give a series of ten lectures between 29 April and 19

May on changing understandings of the City of God and (2) dedicate the Cardinal Mercier Chair at the University of Louvain.

On 22 September, Gilson was back in Canada to represent the Académie Française for the centenary celebration of the University of Laval and to receive an honorary doctorate from Laval. He spoke there about the first French book published in Canada, in 1765: Msgr. Jean-Joseph Lenguet's *Catéchisme du diocese de Sens.*

On 06 October he presented a paper entitled "Education and Higher Learning" as the inaugural address for St. Michael's College's centennial. In this paper, among other things, Gilson criticized the tendency of modern democratic governments to present education as if it were a commodity.

On 05 March, 1953, Gilson delivered a paper entitled "Thomas Aquinas and Our Colleagues" to the Aquinas Foundation in Princeton, New Jersey. This paper was published by the Foundation in 1953 and in 1956 as part of Anton C. Pegis's *A Gilson Reader.*

Gilson had some medical problems in 1953 and did not do any conference presentations again until 26 August, when he spoke on the theme "Remarques sur l'expérience en métaphysique" at the Eleventh International Congress of Philosophy, in Brussels (published the same year in *Acts du XIe congrés international de philosophie*). In 1953, Pegis had asked Gilson to help him establish a Catholic Textbook Division within Doubleday and Company publishers. Gilson spent much of the winter of 1954 with this work. During this time he also wrote for Doubleday a preface to Pope Leo XIII's social encyclicals entitled *The Church Speaks to the Modern World.* Also in 1954, Gilson spent a lot of time preparing the fourth series of the Mellon Lectures to be given in 1955 at the National

Gallery in Washington, DC. In January 1954 Gilson had to give a sample lecture to at the Gallery. He did so on the topic "The Aesthetic Doctrines of Maurice Denis."

On 24 February, 1954, Gilson gave an informal talk on philosophy and art at a Jesuit seminary in Toronto. On 29 April, he presented a paper at Mount St. Vincent College in Halifax, Nova Scotia. Between 20 and 26 June, he participated in the Third Annual Congress for Peace and Christian Culture in Florence. While there he gave a paper on "L'universalisme et la paix." He followed this up between 19 and 22 August with six lectures at the new Centre d'Études Supérieures de Civilisation Médiévale at Poitiers.

During the fall of 1954, Gilson returned to the United States to participate in a conference on the "Unity of Knowledge" at Columbia University and, along with England's Queen Mother Mary and other dignitaries, receive an honorary degree. On 28 October, at Arden House, Gilson presented what Shook has called "one of the most important" papers of Gilson's career, published in 1955 in the book *The Unity of Knowledge* under the title "Theology and the Unity of Knowledge." During the same year, Random House published Gilson's famous *History of Christian Philosophy in the Middle Ages*, and he wrote a preface for Doubleday's textbook edition of John Henry Newman's *Grammar of Assent*. In March and April, Gilson presented his metaphysical analysis of art in six Mellon lectures at the National Gallery in Washington, DC. These lectures were published in the Bollingen Series in 1957 under the title *Painting and Reality*.

With time on his hands for several weeks in Washington, Gilson spoke to seminar philosophy students at the Catholic University of

America. Up to this time, due perhaps to his Sorbonne training and commitment to the French university system, some Catholic University administrators and Dean of the School of Philosophy, Fr. Ignatius Smith, considered Gilson a *persona non grata.* Despite a somewhat critical introduction of Gilson by Smith, according to Shook, Gilson used the opportunity to "produce one of the major classroom performances of his life" to about 750 people who had packed Catholic University's McMahon Auditorium.

While also doing other things, during the summer, 1955, Gilson wrote an introduction for a Doubleday textbook edition of St. Augustine's *Confessions.* He followed this with an October lecture on education in Cleveland. On 27 March, 1956, Gilson, engaged in a radio interview for station CKAC, Montreal.

On 14 April, he flew out of New York to spend two months in Bogota, Colombia and São Paulo, Brazil. He gave twenty-one lectures in twelve days at nine universities in Bogota and six lectures in nine days in São Paulo, chiefly on the topic "Being According to St. Thomas Aquinas"—interspersed at times with some reflections on "tableaux et existence" and "The Labyrinth of Painting." Gilson returned to France during the second week in June so that he could attend a meeting of the Académie Française and then fly to Bonn, Germany to receive "Der Orden Pour le Mérite für Wissenschafte und Kunste."

During the summer of 1956, Gilson gave a course of six lectures in Poitiers. He also started to prepare a paper for the Roman Academy of St. Thomas Aquinas entitled "Sur deux themes de réflexion." The paper was published in a 1957 volume, *Omaggio*, written by Fr. Charles Boyer and dedicated to Pope Pius

XII. Starting in 1957 Gilson began to turn down most invitations to give outside lectures. He made exceptions that year for: (1) two unpaid talks given in February to the Alliance Française of Montreal; and (2) in early September for the twelfth "Rencontre Internationale de Genève" (an annual conference that had grown out of the UN UNESCO and Hague meetings in which Gilson had participated). At the colloquium Gilson spoke to the conference theme, "L'Europe et la liberation de l'art," a topic that might have been generated by his Mellon lectures.

During this same year, he accepted an invitation: (1) from the American Academy of Arts and Sciences to become a member of a board of twelve scholars for a new quarterly journal: *Daedalus*; and (2) from the Faculty of Theology at the University of Freiburg-im-Breisgau to accept an honorary degree. He also wrote three important articles: (1) "What is Christian Philosophy?"; (2) "Le centenaire d'Auguste Comte" (published in *Le monde* for the centenary celebration of Comte's death); and (3) "Amicus amicis" (an address to students preparing an "Etienne Gilson Tribute" [Milwaukee, 1959]). In the spring, 1957, Gilson was named general editor for a four-volume textbook on the *History of Philosophy*. He also had to fill in as a contributing editor. He left for Canada early in January, 1958, and did not return to North America until the winter of 1959.

On 05 May 1958, Gilson was named a "Membre de l'Académie Royale de Belgique, Section des Sciences Morales et Politiques." Also in May, he finished an article he called "Autour du thomisme," the substance of which he later presented in a recorded lecture for the Pontifical Institute under the title "The Future of Christian Philosophy." In June, he wrote the main article on Gabriel Marcel's reception of "Le Prix National," entitled "Un philosophe singulier" and published in *Les nouvelles litteraires.* And on 18 September he presented a paper on "L'oeuvre d'art et le jugement critique," at the "Symposium d'Esthétiques" in Venice. During the time of this same Symposium, Gilson spoke at the Cini Foundation about Pietro Pomponazzi's teaching on the immortality of the soul in a paper entitled, "L'affaire de l"immortalité de l'âge à Venice au début du XVIe siècle" (published in 1964 in *Umanesimo europeo e umanesimo veneziano*).

Gilson underwent surgery in January 1959. This left him convalescing until spring. Still, he managed to write an "In Memoriam" tribute for the *Archives* regarding the death of Gabriel Théry; and, upon request, between March and December, he fulfilled functions of the Académie Française. In November, he traveled to Brussels and gave two public lectures for the Faculté Universitaire Saint-Louis: (1) "Un théologien devant les philosophes: St. Thomas d'Aquin" and (2) "Un philosophe devant les théologiens: Henri Bergson."

During this visit to Brussels he was inducted into the Royal Academy of Belgium. For the occasion, he gave an hour-long, spellbinding talk on "Philosophie du Plagiat" ("The Philosophy of Plagiarism"). On 21 November, 1959, Gilson chaired the meeting of "La Semaine des Intellectuels Catholiques" in Paris. The two speakers were Père M.-D. Chenu and M. Jean Lacroix. Shook reports that, in his summation of this discussion, "Gilson presented his last refined judgment on theology in relation to the thought of man. He came very near to saying that, for the believer, philosophy in the generally accepted sense of the word is an impossibility. He also offered one of the best explanations of why he now insisted so adamantly that St. Thomas had been a theologian who had used philosophy as a theologian" (Gilson's summation appears in *Semaines des Intellectuels Catholiques*, Paris, 1959).

Shook adds: Gilson, then, had come to see theology as the meeting place of reason and the Christian mystery seeking understanding of itself: "*haec creendo, incipe, procurre, persiste . . . intellige incomprehensibilia esse. . . .* Gilson, grown in this faith and its mysteries, hoped that he had become, like Thomas, a theologian. Had he dared, he would have called *Le philosophe* (Note: that is, he would have called his book (*Le philosophe et la théologie*): "*Le théologien et la philosophie.*"

In honor of his seventy-fifth birthday Gilson was gratified to receive three festschrifts from former students: (1) a 1959 volume of *Medieval Studies* dedicated to him and containing articles by his Toronto colleagues; (2) thirty-four papers, with the exception of one, all by Europeans, edited by Alex Denomy, simultaneously published by Vrin and PIMS, appearing under the title Mélanges offerts à Étienne Gilson; and (3) a collective volume of papers written and edited by North American students entitled *An Étienne Gilson Tribute*. Gilson included his own tribute to the wisdom of Pegis in this volume, entitling it,"Amicus amicis."

From around Christmas 1959, Gilson started working with his daughter Cécile to translate *Le philosophe et la théologie* into English. (It eventually saw publication in 1961 under the title *The Philosopher and Theology*.) For the next three years he also tried to resolve problems related to completing his four-volume *History of Philosophy*. This second project brought him to New York City for a meeting in early April at Random House publishers. This allowed him the opportunity, on 07 April 1959, to go to Hartford, Connecticut, to give a McAuley Lecture at St. Joseph College on the topic "Can the Existence of God be Demonstrated?" (published in 1961 in *St. Thomas and Philosophy*).

On 07 March 1960, Gilson spoke at Rockhurst College, Kansas City, on "Paths to Peace." An English translation of Gilson's paper dedicated to Pope Pius XII ("Sur deux themes de réflexion") and this talk at Rockhurst would later become the first and last chapters of Gilson's 1964 book, *The Spirit of Thomism.*

In addition to publishing *The Philosopher and Theology* in 1961, in that year he also published his articles, "Trois leçons sur le problème de l'existence du Dieu" (in *Divinitas*) and "Du la connaissance du principe" (in Revuede métaphysique et de morale). During the summer, 1961, Gilson gave a short lecture in Bolzano, Italy. And he planned to give a fall course on "An Introduction to the Theology of St. Thomas Aquinas" at the Harvard Divinity School. In a letter to Armand A. Maurer, Gilson even quipped that he would "enjoy speaking of a theologian without having to conceal that he is a theologian." Health problems, including surgery, however, prevented him from giving this class. In 1962, Gilson published "Il problema dell'ateismo," based upon an article he had written entitled, "La possibilité de l'athéisme," "L'être et Dieu" (in *Revue thomiste*), some articles in *Mediaeval Studies*, and his second edition of *L'être et l'essence*."

Gilson went from France to Canada toward the end of January 1963 and stayed until May 1964. While in North America, aside from his courses at the Institute, he gave six public lectures, many based upon his 1963 book, *Introduction aux arts du beau*. He followed up this book with his 1964 book on the fine arts: *Matières et formes*.

On 03 March, 1963, he gave an Institute seminar on "Prolegomena to the *Prima via*" (published in *Archives*, 1963); on 09 May, he spoke at the Institute convocation on the topic, "Research Schools in the Context of St. Thomas on Education." In early November, he spoke at Carr Hall, Toronto, on "The Birth of the Lutheran Reformation." After returning to France, from 11 to 13 November, 1963, Gilson gave six lectures to the monks of the Abbaye Saint Benoit de Fleury at Saint-Benoit-sur-Loire. On 13 December, he participated in a public homage to Père A. D. Sertillanges in his talk, "Souvenir du Père Sertillanges."

Gilson ended 1963 upset by news that Burt Franklin had announced in New York a reprint of Gilson's 1913 *Index scolastico-cartesian*. Gilson had not authorized the reprint and had refused money for the rights to republish it because he did not consider the complementary dissertation a complete work of scholarship.

After Gilson returned to Canada in mid-February 1964, between 28 February and 20 March, he gave four lectures at the Institute on "The Spirit of Thomism." In revised form, he repeated these lectures in April for the 175th Anniversary of the founding of Georgetown University. He would later use these same talks as part of the foundation for his 1964 book *The Spirit of Thomism*. Shortly before going to Georgetown, Gilson spoke in Toronto to the University College Literary and Athletic Society" on the theme "On Moral Progress."

In early September, 1964, Gilson again returned to the Georgio Cini Foundation in Venice to give three talks on the plastic arts, music, and writing, entitled "Industrialization of the Arts" (published in 1966 in *Arte e cultura nella civilian contemporanea*). Partly under the influence of talks he had had with Marshall McLuhan at the Institute and the Communications Centre at the University of Toronto, Gilson extended his analysis of the fine arts in light of the effects of technology on them. Gilson returned to Canada in November, 1964, to give four lectures from late November until early December at the Royal Ontario Museum on: (1) "Luther's Starting Point; (2) "Personal Experiences and Theology"; (3) "The Freedom of a Christian"; and (4) "The Fly and the Elephant."

Returning to Europe in early January, 1965, Gilson remained there until October of the same year. One reason he stayed in Europe so long was to help him defend Thomism against growing assaults from theologians and liturgists who were trying to reduce Thomism's in Church life. During this time he published his sixth, and last, edition of *Le Thomisme*. He also revised and presented several versions of a talk, "St. Thomas et nous" (one of which he gave in Rome on 13 April). On 06 September, he gave the only paper at the Solemn Inauguration of the Sixth International Thomistic Congress in Rome: "De la notion de l'être divin dans la philosophie de Sainte Thomas d'Aquin."

During the same year he also published an article "Trois leçons sur le thomisme et sa situation prèsente" (in *Seminarium*). Gilson was especially pleased when, at a reception for the members of the Congress at Castel Gandolfo, Pope Paul VI said, "Thomas is, was, and always will be the *Doctor Communis* . . . the master of all and for all" in the Church.

On 02 July, Gilson published an article entitled "Suis-je schismatique?" in La France catholique in which he objected to the replacement in the French version of the Mass that the Son is "consubstantial" with the Father with the phrase Son is "of the same nature" as motivated by the modern mind's rejection of the notion of "substance."

In 1965, in preparation for the seventh centenary of Dante Aligheri's birth, Gilson published in *Archives*, under the title "Trois études dantesque," three previously written papers: (1)"Dante's 'Mirabile Visione'"; (2) "What is a Shade?"; and (3) "Poetry and Theology in The Divine Comedy." He lectured on one or more of these papers in Florence (21 April), Montreal (29 October), Cornell (01 and 02 November), Toronto (05, 15, and 19 November), Berkeley, Augsburg, and other places. He also published an article entitled "À la recherché de l'Émpyrée" in the *Revue des etudes italiennes*.

In September, 1965, Gilson lectured: (1) for Count Cini in Milan about "L'industrialization des belles letters"; (2) in Rome, Turin, Naples, and, with variations, in Soisy-sous-Étoiles on "Saint Thomas et nous."

Gilson spent much of 1966 in France preparing fall lectures for Toronto and taking care of personal business. Before leaving for Toronto in October, he gave a paper to all five "Académies de l'Institut de France" on what he published the same year under the title "Les arts et les letters." Gilson arrived in Toronto in the fall of 1966 with seven articles. Six related to "The Renewal of Metaphysics." The seventh was a historical paper on "The Cultural Revolution of the Thirteenth Century." Gilson delivered one to three of the six metaphysical papers at the Institute, St. Joseph's College in West Hartford, Connecticut, Assumption College in Windsor, Ontario, and to other institutions. On 05 January, 1967, he gave his historical paper as part of the Distinguished Lecture Series, at the University of New Hampshire, Durham (the article was published in 1968 as part of that Series).

In 1967, Gilson was quite busy. In February, he received an honorary degree at the University of Bologna. On 11 May, he spoke at the Pantheon for the unveiling of a tablet in honor of Henri Bergson. On 29 May, he was in Berlin for a week where he attended the annual chapter of the "Orden Pouur le Mérite." He limited his work in Canada to participation in the: (1) International Congress on the Theology of Renewal, Pontifical Institute of Mediaeval Studies, Toronto, 02 to 25 August (at which he presented a paper entitled "On Behalf of the Handmaid" [published in 1968 in Lawrence K. Shook (ed.), *Theology of Renewal*]); and (2) Fourth International Congress of Medieval Philosophy, Montreal, immediately after the PIMS conference (at which Gilson spoke about "The Liberal Arts and Philosophy in the Middle Ages"). On 06 November, he received an honorary degree from the University of Liège. On 15 November, he participated in a radio tribute to Jacques Maritain.

During the same year, Gilson published two articles in the *Essais d'art et de philosophie*: (1) "La société de masse et sa culture" and (2) "Les tribulations de Sophie." Between 23 February and 16 March 1968, Gilson lectured in Toronto on problems related to atheism: (1)

"The Problem of the Non-Existence of God: The Difficulties of Atheism"; (2) "Is God Dead?"; (3) "The True Problem"; and (4) "Is the Non-Existence of God Even Thinkable?"

Shook claims that Gilson had intended to do a major work on atheism and the idea of God, intending to call the to-be-published book "Constanes philosophiques de l'être." While he never completed this work, after Gilson died, his friend Henri Gouhier made parts of the contents available in the 1979 book *L'atheisme difficile*.

Before returning to Toronto in 1969, Gilson took a detour to Berkeley, where he arrived on 03 January to give two courses, one public, one specialized seminar, at the University. His public lecture, based upon the *Summa theologiae*, was on the authentic Thomism of St. Thomas. His seminar was devoted to texts of Avicenna and St. Thomas.

Back in Toronto after three days in San Francisco, Gilson gave three lectures entitled: (1) "Language is Metaphysical"; (2) "Words and Meanings"; and (3) "Poetry and Metaphysics." From 09 to 15 April, 1969, Gilson was scheduled to be at the Accademia dei Lincei of Rome to participate in a symposium entitled "Oriental and Occidental Medieval Philosophy and Science" and to give a paper there on "Avicenne en occident au moyen âge." While he wound up not attending, Thérèse d'Alverny presented "a compendium" of the talk to which she added a section, "Y-a-t'il eu un avicennisme latin?" (later published in *Archives*).

Throughout 1969 and 1970, Shook reports that some members of Chicago's "Great Books" team had pursued Gilson to help them create a "Library of Mediaeval Civilization" on microfiche. At this time, Shook maintains, "Gilson's position on metaphysics had much in common with that defended by Mortimer J. Adler in *The Difference of Man and the Difference It Makes* (1967)." He adds that, in correspondence with John N. Deely, "Gilson had spoken favourably of Adler's 'long first step toward the proper assessment of an immaterial element in material reality.'"

Gilson devoted his 1970 lecture series in Toronto to the general topic, "Finalism Revisited." The series consisted of four lectures: "The Case for Mechanical Causality," "The Case for the Mechanical Cause," "Finalism and Physical Probability," and "Evolution: Teleology and Theology." In 1971, Gilson published the material contained in these lectures in his book *D'Aristote à Darwin et retour*. In December 1970, he also gave a paper entitled "Propose sur le bonheur" to the Académie Française.

The general topic of Gilson's 1970 Toronto lecture series apparently generated the general topic for his 1971 and 1972 series. Gilson gave his 1971 series the general title, "In Quest of Evolution." This series consisted of three lectures: "Darwin without Evolution," "Evolution without Darwin," and "From Malthus to the Twilight of Evolution." He gave the 1972 series (his last series of lectures in Toronto) the general title, "In Quest of Species." This series also consisted of three lectures: "Species for Experience," "Species for Science," and "Species for Philosophy." Among other things, within these lectures, Gilson expressed appreciation to Adler for pointing "out the mistake of those scholastics who confuse logical with biological species." He added, "True species are found in zoos. There are no other." And "[Aristotle] merely says: 'No part of an animal is purely material or purely immaterial.' Drop the immaterial and the notion of species makes no sense. It is not a scientific notion, but a philosophical one."

Prior to giving his 1972 lectures in Toronto, under persistent pressure from the Dean of the School of Philosophy, Jude P. Dougherty, President Clarence C. Walton of the Catholic University of America invited Gilson to receive an honorary degree as Doctor of Human Letters from the University on 15 May 1971. While Dougherty was unable to get the president to invite Gilson to give the convocation address, he was able to exert enough pressure to have the University pay Gilson's airfare. And Dougherty arranged for Gilson to give a "post-commencement" address in Keane Auditorium to a diverse audience of listeners from all over the Washington, DC area.

On 07 March 1972, the Brazilian Academy of the Latin World awarded Gilson the Gulbenkian prize for philosophy in Paris. On 30 July 1972, he completed three more lectures that he had intended to give in Toronto the next academic year. The general topic of these lectures was "In Quest of Matter." It consisted of three methods of considering matter, the: (1) ancient Greek, (2) Christian philosophical, and (3) "scientific" method followed after Descartes. His age and weakened health did not permit him to go to Toronto to present the lectures.

Even though Gilson's health continued to weaken, in 1973 he wrote a four-page introduction for John Osty's translation of *The Book of Wisdom*. In September 1973, Thérèse d'Alverny and Pierre de Paulhac suggested for Gilson to publish some of his papers on Dante not readily known in France. This suggestion produced Gilson's 1974 book, *Dante et Béatrice: études dantesques*.

On 11 November 1973, Gilson gave an address over French radio on "la patrie." In 1974, Gilson was pleased to see in print his article on "Quasi definitio substantia" (published by PIMS under the general editorship of Armand A. Maurer in the septicenteniary, 2 volume, edition commemorating St. Thomas's death: *St. Thomas Aquinas, 1274–1974, Commemorative Studies.*

Gilson spent his remaining years in the village of Cravant, France. During this time he received many visitors. On one occasion, his friend Henri Gouhier, a Commander in *La Légion d'Honneur*, conferred on Gilson the insignia of the "ordre pouré le Mérite." On 20 February 1975, Gilson traveled to Paris, where the Académie de France conferred on him the gold medal they give to members who have reached at least the age of 90.

In September, 1978, then age 95, Gilson moved from his house in Cravant to the Centre Hospitalier in Auxerre. While he continued to weaken physically, he remained intellectually alert and talkative until his death on 19 September 1978. His funeral Mass was said at La Cathédrale de Saint-Étienne in Auxerre. He is buried beside his wife, Thérèse, in the cemetery of Melun.

In her *Étienne Gilson: A Bibliography, Une Bibliographie* (Toronto: Pontifical Institute of Mediaeval Studies, 1982), Margaret McGrath (ed.) reports that, during his intellectual life, Gilson's known publications amounted to 935 works: 172 monographs, 8 edited books, 4 series editions, 2 anthologies, 307 scholarly articles, 36 prefaces, 296 general interest articles, 104 book reviews. A brief online bibliography of Gilson's work is available at: http://academie-francaise.fr/immortels/index.htm.[1]

[1]Another valuable bibliographical resource for Gilson studies is Callistus James Edie, "The Writings of Étienne Gilson, Chronologically Arranged," in *Mélanges offerts à Étienne Gilson* (Toronto: Pontifical Institute of Mediaeval Studies and Paris, J. Vrin, 1959), 15–58. Except for a few minor additions, all the content in the above Biography is derived from Lawrence K. Shook's Gilson biography entitled, *Étienne Gilson* (Toronto, Pontifical Institute of Mediaeval Studies, The Gilson Series 6, 1984).

Chapter 2

Why Gilson? Why Now?[1]

Before I start my talk, I want to thank all of you who have taken the time to join us today in Warsaw for this historic founding of the International Étienne Gilson Society. I wish to talk to you today about why, at this precise time in history, founding an international Etienne Gilson Society is crucial to recovering in the West today proper understandings of human nature and of philosophy and why without recovering these proper understandings, within a short time, we will not be able to heal growing cultural antagonisms within the West and Western culture will likely fall victim to a new form of totalitarianism.

In 1990, just after the fall of the Berlin Wall and the concordist euphoria that was sweeping Western Europe, I presented a paper at a prestigious, and first, international colloquium on the new world order "Transition in Eastern Europe" in Italy. This meeting was co-hosted in Treviso, Italy (just north of Venice) by the Konrad Adenauer Stiftung and the Instituto Internazionale Jacques Maritain at the latter's Villa Franchetti. Since attendees at this meeting included

[1] This chapter was first published in Issue 1 (2012) in the first volume of the philosophical and classical journal *Studia Gilsoniana* to commemorate the founding in Poland of the International Étienne Gilson Society. I thank the current editor-in-chief of *Studia Gilsoniana*, Imelda Chłodna-Błach for granting me permission to republish it here in its slightly revised form.

new world order globalist leaders from different European parliaments, university dons, and international corporate leaders (including the president of the Bank of Rome), its perimeter was surrounded by armed guards carrying Uzzi machine guns and walking German Shepherd guard dogs.

As vice president of the American Maritain Association (AMA), I was invited to represent the AMA by presenting a paper at this world congress. Being still somewhat young (45 years old) and somewhat naive at the time, thinking that the organizers would be interested in hearing what I thought Maritain would have said had he been there, I entitled my paper "The New World Disorder." In it I argued that, instead of being signs of growing world concord, the transitions then occurring in Europe were “readily recognizable as convulsions within the Western conception of man.”

Instead of attempting to restore the West through such misguided means as economic theory and politics, I held that only a complete purging of Western cultural institutions of the Cartesian understanding of human nature would be able to restore Western culture to health. If this view of the human self continued to dominate Western culture, I predicted that: (1) the West would “self-destruct in a cultural collapse” and (2) “this collapse will, in all probability, be issued in by new and more exotic forms of fundamentalistic political perversions of the totalitarian state attempting to unify human society around monolithic myths of the race, mechanistic reason, blind evolution, materialistic progress, and so on."[2]

Just after doing so, much to his chagrin, the representative of the Konrad Adenauer Stiftung stood up, *screamed at me several times to "shut up," and cut off my speaking time*. Apparently, my talk had ruined his globalist dream of announcing at this colloquium the realization of Francis Fukuyama's musings that the world had finally reached the *End of History*, in which secular liberalism, as the best of all possible governments, would finally bring about global peace.

In reaction to his boorish behavior, I apologized to my audience for not being able to finish my talk and sat down. Immediately, audience members gave me a standing ovation; and as I exited the stairs to leave the stage, they surrounded me, peppered me with questions.

The reason I could so confidently make these predictions is not mysterious. Decades ago, I had the good fortune to read Gilson's *The Unity of Philosophical Experience*.[3] In this work, Gilson outlined how, since the dawn of the modern world in the seventeenth century, Western culture had started to engage in a reckless adventure to abandon the Greek philosophical vision of the universe. Gilson called this Greek philosophical vision the "Western Creed," and he saw it as the essential foundation of all Western cultural institutions.

---

[2] For a more detailed treatment of the new world order as a kind of anti-philosophical disorder, see Peter A. Redpath, "The New World Disorder: A Crisis of Philosophical Identity," in *Contemporary Philosophy*, 16:6 (November/December 1994), 19–24.

[3] Étienne Gilson, *The Unity of Philosophical Experience* (New York: Charles Scribner's Sons, repr. 1965 of original 1937 Charles Scribner's Sons publication).

Simultaneous with the West's attempt to abandon the Western Creed, Gilson saw the West attempting to replace the Greek philosophical vision with something Gilson called the "Scientific Creed." As far back as the 1930s Gilson was pointing to Cartesian thought as a cultural revolution that had attempted to reduce all philosophy, sense realism, and science to the practical mechanistic science of mathematical physics. In ancient times philosophy and science were considered identical. And philosophical sciences like metaphysics, ethics, and politics could make claims to have a foundation for their principles in the sense world, in a sense realism, sense wonder. All these sciences could claim, in some way, to be rational, realistic, true.

After Descartes and the Protestant Reformation had come on the scene, Gilson thought that something had been radically altered in the relationship between modern mathematical physics and the classical sciences of metaphysics, ethics, and politics. Just like the Protestant Reformers Martin Luther and John Calvin, Descartes showed a distrust for natural reason. Despite the fact that Descartes is celebrated for his declaration that truth lies in "clear and distinct ideas," Descartes had actually located all human truth and error in strength and weakness of the human will, in what Friedrich Nietzsche would famously later identify as the "Will to Power."

As Descartes saw the human condition, we human beings are spirits encased in machines. We are essentially two substances that cannot communicate with each other. God is the only cause of communication between these two substances, our mind and body. Hence, for Descartes the proper object of human science is clear and distinct ideas, not real, or mind-independent, beings that we grasp with the help of our bodily senses. Moreover, Descartes thought "science" is a name that we give to different logical deductive systems of clear and distinct ideas. Descartes reduced all philosophy, science, to differing kinds of systematic logic.

Outside restraints placed upon the human imagination by reasoning systematically under the influence of clear and distinct ideas like God, the soul, and extension, Descartes thought our unrestrained imaginations tended to cause our wills to wander, to become weak and unable to focus on ideas, see them clearly, grasp truth, and provide us with true science. In the area of physical science, Descartes maintained that just this sort of wandering occurs when we try to determine the essence of the sense world independently of the use of mathematical ideas. Hence, for Descartes, because it uses clear and distinct ideas to view the sense universe, mathematical physics is the only science that can tell us anything true about the essence of the sense world. And because they use clear and distinct ideas to study human freedom, while human sciences like metaphysics, politics, and ethics can tell us something true about the human spirit, they can tell us nothing true about the existence and use of freedom in the sensible world.[4]

Within a century and a half of Descartes's dream of re-establishing science on the foundation of a system of clear and distinct ideas, and after the wondrous success of Newtonian physics, the Lutheran thinker Immanuel Kant sought to go beyond Descartes and simultaneously protect the fundamentalistic Lutheran understanding of

---

[4] For a detailed exposition and critique of Descartes's teachings about philosophy and science, see Peter A. Redpath, *Cartesian Nightmare: An Introduction to Transcendental Sophistry* (Amsterdam and Atlanta: Editions Rodopi, B. V., 1997).

faith by effectively divorcing philosophical discip-lines of metaphysics, politics, and ethics completely from science and sense reality and reducing all scientific reasoning and sense realism to mechanistic mathematical physics.[5] By so doing, Kant solidified a divorce that Descartes had introduced between truth and freedom, faith and science, and the philosophical disciples of metaphysics, ethics, and politics from contemporary mathematical physics, science, and sense reality.

At present, this several-hundred year project to divorce philosophy from science and reduce science to mechanized mathematical physics has created an essential conflict within Western cultural institutions, within our intellectual, political, and religious organizations. In Cartesian thought, truth and freedom are properties of will, not reason. Hence, freedom and truth are essentially non-rational. And rationality is essentially not free or true. This means that, while modern physical science might wish to make claims to truth, if it claims to be rational, it can only make true statements when by "true statements" we mean statements expressing non-rational feelings or "beliefs." Truth in Cartesian science can be no more than an intense feeling about an idea or system of ideas. Hence the propensity of so many thinkers today to refer to physical science as a "belief system."

This essential opposition between reason and will, freedom, and truth means that, within a Cartesian conception of science, we can never be free by acting rationally because free behavior is essentially

---

[5] For a detailed exposition and critique of the role Kant played in the Cartesian revolution, see Peter A. Redpath, *Masquerade of the Dream Walkers: Prophetic Theology from the Cartesians to Hegel* (Amsterdam and Atlanta, Editions Rodopi, B. V., 1998), 101–166.

non-rational. Hence the propensity of so many Western youth today to identify being free with doing "crazy" things. Moreover, this essential opposition between of reason and will, freedom, and truth means that, within a Cartesian conception of science we have totally abdicated any means for rationally judging, evaluating, truth in any of our intellectual, cultural, or political institutions or disciplines. Hence the rampant madness, falsehood, and dishonesty that increasingly infect Western cultural institutions (like universities, politics, media, business, sports) in their essential operations.

After all, if we buy into the Cartesian worldview, if we want to be scientifically political, politically truthful, we cannot expect to behave reasonably. And if we want to be politically rational we cannot expect to say anything true. If we want to scientifically intellectual, we have to express our feelings. And these feelings have to be intensely non-rational if we expect them to express any truth, and not truthful if we expect them to be in any way rational. If we want to be successful, behave reasonably, in business, sports, or media, we have to lie and be dishonest because the rational is the opposite of what is true.

Given the essential madness of Cartesian thought, over the past several centuries, Western thinkers have attempted to use several intellectual frauds, different forms of sophistry, to help maintain the intellectually unjustifiable modern reduction of all science to physics and the divorce of truth and freedom from rationality. Chief among these frauds has been modern socialism, which has called upon neo-gnostic thinkers like Georg Hegel, Karl Marx, and Charles Darwin and pseudo-politicians like Adolf Hitler, Benito Mussolini, and Josef Stalin to fabricate the myth that the essential flaw within modern

Western Cartesian thought has actually been a necessary historical moment in the march of the human spirit to emerge from some form of backward historical consciousness into that of an Enlightened socialism bringing into being a new scientific world order.

Shortly after the end of World War II, Gilson wrote a powerful work entitled *The Terrors of the Year 2000* in which he predicted that, instead of learning its cultural lesson about the need to reconcile the divorce between classical philosophy and modern physical science, the post-World War II era would yield no lasting peace and would become a time "where science, formerly our hope and our joy, would be the source of greatest terror."[6]

At the close of World War II, Gilson claimed, with the help of Nietzsche, we human beings brought the modern conflict between rationality and truth and freedom to a new level. With the bombing of Hiroshima, we in the West had made our most astounding scientific discovery: "the great secret that science has just wrested from matter is the secret of its destruction. To know today is synonymous with to destroy."[7]

With Nietzsche's short sentence, "They do not know that God is dead," Gilson thought that the transvaluation of Western values had started in earnest. Postmodern man wished to make himself divine, usurp God's place, become God. Gilson considered Nietzsche's declaration of God's death "the capital discovery of modern times." Compared to Nietzsche's discovery, Gilson maintained that, no

---

[6] Étienne Gilson, *The Terrors of the Year 2000* (Toronto: St. Michael's College, 1949), 5, 7.

[7] Gilson, *The Terrors of the Year* 2000, 7–9.

matter how far back we trace human history, we "will find no upheaval to compare with this in the extent or in the depth of its cause." Gilson thought that Nietzsche's declaration of God's death signaled a metaphysical revolution of the highest, widest, and deepest order.[8]

From time immemorial, Gilson thought we in the West have based our cultural creed and scientific inspiration, our intellectual and cultural institutions, upon our Western Creed, which included the conviction that gods, or a God, existed. No longer. All of a sudden, God no longer exists. Worse, He never existed! For Gilson the implication is clear: "We shall have to change completely our every thought, word and deed. The entire human order totters on its base."[9]

If our entire cultural history depended upon the unswerving conviction that God exists, "the totality of the future must needs depend on the contrary certitude, that God does not exist," on a subliminal hatred of the Western Creed. Gilson thought that Nietzsche's message was a metaphysical bomb more powerful than the atomic weapon dropped on Hiroshima: "Everything that was true from the beginning of the human race will suddenly become false." Moreover, mankind alone must create for itself a new self-definition, which will become human destiny, the human project: To destroy.[10]

Gilson maintained that Nietzsche's discovery of God's death signaled the dawn of a new age, a new political world disorder, in which

---

[8] Gilson, *The Terrors of the Year* 2000, 14–16. Gilson cites Nietzsche's "Ecce Homo," especially "Why I am a Fatality."

[9] Gilson, *The Terrors of the Year* 2000, 14–16.

[10] Gilson, *The Terrors of the Year* 2000, 16–17.

the aim of postmodern culture, its metaphysical project, had become to make war upon, to overthrow, traditional truths and values. To build our brave new world order, we have to go beyond Descartes and overthrow the metaphysical foundations of Western culture. "Before stating what will be true, we will have to say that everything by which man has thus far lived, everything by which he still lives, is deception and trickery." As Nietszche says, "He who would be a creator, both in good and evil, must first of all know how to destroy and to wreck values." The new world disorder is one in which we are busy "preparing the brave new world of tomorrow by first of all annihilating the world of today."[11]

As Gilson saw it, postmodern man, the man of the new world order, is essentially Nietzschean. And his "mad ambition," to become totally free of any external moral restraints on moral or political behavior, is impossible to achieve.[12] We might wish to become absolutely free creators, creators ex nihilo, totally free, but, at best, our wish is an impossible dream. "We shall perhaps be great manufacturers," Gilson says. "[B]ut creators—never. To create in his turn ex nihilo, man must first of all reestablish everywhere the void."[13]

Mad ambition, then, has become postmodern man's project: everywhere to reestablish the void, a new world disorder, by wrecking traditional Western values. Gilson sees this Nietzschean project to be a continuation of the Enlightenment project, to create a utopian new world order in which, against the backward intellectual and moral traditions of Jews, Christians, and ancient philosophers,

---

[11] Gilson, *The Terrors of the Year* 2000, 17–18.

[12] Gilson, *The Terrors of the Year* 2000, 17.

[13] Gilson, *The Terrors of the Year* 2000, 18–20.

the mad dreams of the poetic human imagination and utopian socialists replace reality.

The new world disorder is universal surrealism, total release of human reason, of creative free spirit, from all traditional metaphysical, moral, and aesthetic controls; the poetic spirit, the spirit of the artist gone totally mad with the intoxicating, surrealistic power of destruction. Gilson maintained that the father of post-modern man's post-World War II existential project is Sisyphus. Our destiny has become "the absurd" and "truly exhausting task" of perpetual self-invention without model, purpose, or rule. Having turned ourselves into gods, we do not know what to do with our divinity.[14] Finding ourselves totally free to engage in the perpetual task of endless self-creation, Gilson said we resemble a soldier on a twenty-four hour leave with nothing to do: totally bored in the tragic loneliness of an idle freedom we cannot productively use.[15]

Gilson considered our postmodern story to be really quite old. Like the Jewish people in the time of Samuel, tired of being really free, we seek expand our freedom by putting ourselves under the rule of a king.[16] Having freed ourselves from divine rule, the necessary political consequence for postmodern man is political enslavement by a totalitarian State. Having refused to serve God, we have no one left to judge the State, no arbiter between us and the State.[17]

To Gilson's ears, the explosion of Hiroshima resounded a solemn metaphysical assertion of postmodern man's statement that,

---

[14]Gilson, *The Terrors of the Year* 2000, 21–25.

[15]Gilson, *The Terrors of the Year* 2000, 24.

[16]Gilson, *The Terrors of the Year* 2000, 26–27; *Book of Samuel* (8:7–22).

[17]Gilson, *The Terrors of the Year* 2000, 26–28.

while we no longer want to be God's image, we can still be God's caricature. While we cannot create anything, we now possess the intoxicating power to destroy everything. As a result, feeling totally empty and alone, postmodern man offers, to anyone willing to take it, the futile freedom he does not know how to use. "He is ready for all the dictators, leaders of these human herds who follow them as guides and who are all finally conducted by them to the same place—the *abbatoir*" (the slaughterhouse).[18]

At present, we in Western culture find ourselves in a condition of cultural confusion precisely because, as Gilson understood, we have lost our sense realism and have turned our understanding of science into an enemy of truth and a friend cultural destruction. Having lost our sense realism we have lost our philosophical minds, our philosophical minds have lost touch with reality and have developed a subliminal hatred for our cultural traditions and institutions. Having lost our understanding of the nature of philosophy, we can no longer find any rational arguments by which to justify and sustain our different cultural institutions, which, increasingly we are encouraged to loathe. Having become so completely lost intellectually, we have increasingly transformed ourselves into universal skeptics, prime subjects for enslavement by dictators.

Western culture has traditionally justified its cultural institutions by use of classical philosophical arguments rooted in the common philosophical convictions that man is a rational animal and God exists. Having lost our faith in these essential precepts of the Western Creed, we in the West have largely lost our ability to think

[18]Gilson, *The Terrors of the Year* 2000, 28–29.

philosophically. Thus, we can no longer rationally and philosophically justify Western culture itself.

Why Gilson? Why now? Because, among all the leading intellectuals of the past or present generation no one has better diagnosed the philosophical ills of Western culture and better understood the remedy for those ills than has Gilson. Decades ago Gilson asked a very sobering question for our time: "Can a social order, begotten by a common faith in the value of certain principles, keep on living when all faith in these principles is lost?"[19] Gilson answered this question in the negative. He told us we were losing our freedom because we were "looking at irrationality as the last bulwark of liberty."[20] We were looking to ground human freedom and Western culture on the corpse, and subliminal hatred, of the Western Creed, including the corpse of Western philosophy.

Unhappily, as Gilson has shown us through repeated appeals to philosophical experience, trying to build a social order on the carcass of philosophy is doomed to fail because it ignores "The First Law of Philosophical Experience": "Philosophy always buries its undertakers."[21] This is true whether the undertakers be individuals, politicians, religions, or whole cultures. Since postmodernity's chief problem is that we have lost our reason because we have lost our sense realism, philosophy, and God, Gilson thought that the solution to our ills to be simple. We will not find our reason again until we have "first found God again." And we will not find God again

---

[19]Gilson, *The Unity of Philosophical Experience*, 272.

[20]Gilson, *The Unity of Philosophical Experience*, 293.

[21]Gilson, *The Unity of Philosophical Experience*, 306.

without the willingness "to receive what still remains of grace today."[22] To do that, we must turn our minds again to the world, to have them measured by the being of things, not by our unbridled and unmoored poetic imaginations.

To Gilson, this meant that, to recover our culture, we would have to attempt once again to inhabit the universe of St. Thomas in which the service of God and reason are compatible and produce in us order, beauty, and joy—not nausea—because, in this world, unlike the postmodern Nietzschean world, the necessary condition for the existence of one does not entail the necessary destruction of the other. For, sharing the same cause as part of the same creation, the order of our freedom, thoughts, truth, and, reality complement, they do not contradict, one another. By ignoring the reality that science is principally a habit of mind, not a system, or body of knowledge, and that the being of things constitutes part of philosophy's life-blood, modern "philosophers," including many Thomists, have largely lost our understanding of philosophy as rooted in reality, in principles of sense wonder. In so doing we have all somewhat contributed to a loss of respect for the philosophical realism that underpins the Western Creed that sustains our cultural institutions.

The hour is late. We in the West no longer have the luxury of ignoring a return to philosophical realism and to a philosophical defense of our Western Creed, including our belief in the existence of God. The choice before us is clear: Philosophy or the slaughterhouse, Gilson or Nietzsche. I choose philosophy. Hence, I also choose Gilson. I hope you will join me and my colleagues to help others do the same.

---

[22]Gilson, *The Terrors of the Year* 2000, 29.

Chapter 3

Gilson as Christian Humanist[1]

In chapter 1, paragraph 19, of his encyclical *Caritas in veritate*, quoting Pope Paul VI, Pope Benedict XVI tells us that, among other things, the vision of development as a human vocation today requires "the deep thought and reflection of wise men in search of a new humanism which will enable modern man to find himself anew." In this paper I am going to suggest that the intellectual life of Étienne Gilson constituted just the sort of search for a new humanism about which the Pope speaks, that Gilson's scholarly work was part of a new renaissance—a new humanism that Gilson thought was demanded by the precarious civilizational crisis of the modern West after World Wars I and II. In sum, I wish to argue that, more than anything else, Gilson was a renaissance humanist scholar who consciously worked in the tradition of renaissance humanists before him but did so to expand our understanding of the notion of 'renaissance' scholarship and to create his own brand of Christian humanism to deal with problems distinctive to his age.

---

[1] This chapter was first published in Issue 1(2012) in the first volume of the philosophical and classical journal *Studia Gilsoniana* to commemorate the founding in Poland of the International Étienne Gilson Society. I thank the current editor-in-chief of *Studia Gilsoniana*, Imelda Chłodna-Błach for granting me permission to republish it here in its slightly revised form.

Anyone familiar with the revived interest in Thomistic studies that happened during the late nineteenth and early twentieth centuries will likely be struck by the sharp contrast in writing-style between the manual Thomists who first started this revival and that of Gilson. A chief purpose of this paper is to argue that the radical difference in style is connected in part to a kind of Christian humanism, renaissance way of thinking, that Gilson had developed as part of his distinctive style of doing historical research and of philosophizing.

In referring to Gilson as a 'renaissance humanist,' as did Gilson himself, I am predicating the term 'renaissance' in a wide sense. As is well known, Gilson was chiefly responsible among scholars of the twentieth century for demonstrating as bogus the modern prejudice that attempted to reserve the term 'renaissance' solely to a period of Western intellectual history that had occurred, mainly in Italy, from around AD 1350 to 1600. In my opinion Gilson's critique of this specious intellectual reductionism was part of a conscious attempt on his part to develop his own brand of Christian humanism rooted in a way of philosophizing common to the high Middle Ages. As he saw it, the celebrated Italian renaissance was only one of a series of intellectual renaissances that had occurred in the West prior to the fourteenth century and heavily depended on the scholarly work of many prior centuries.

In referring to Gilson as a humanist, I am predicating the term 'humanist,' in a two-fold way, in accord with two chief ways that I think professional philosophers today generally understand the term "humanism.' In these senses, Gilson the humanist was: (1) a student of classical literary, artistic, and scientific works of Ancient

Greece and Rome. This is the sense in which thinkers such as Paul Oskar Kristeller often use the term to refer to the humanism of the Italian Renaissance. Professional philosophers also use it to refer to: (2) a way of studying that places emphasis on (a) the centrality or dignity of the human person, (b) subjects of study that relate to such centrality or dignity, or (c) ways of engaging in such a study that gives a special dignity to the human subject as agent doing the studying.

Reasonable justification exists to predicate 'humanism' of Gilson's scholarship in both philosophical senses of the term. *Gilsonian humanism has about it the quality of a wonder about the whole of classical wisdom* from the ancient Israelites to the High Middle Ages and beyond; it also emphasizes those subjects that relate to the person's centrality and dignity and the way of studying such subjects such that it gives a special dignity to the agent studying.

In the first sense, similar to the Italian renaissance humanists and many of the renaissance humanists of the high French Middle Ages, including St. Thomas, in the tradition of St. Bernard of Chartres, Gilson engaged in a study of the classics to revive aspects of higher learning in his time, get truth from classical philosophical and theological works, and build upon these truths to see further and deeper than his predecessors.

In the second sense, Gilson's humanism is a way of philosophizing within theology, what Gilson often called a "Christian philosophy." As a Christian theology utilizing the classical mode of philosophizing that traces back to Aristotle, Plato, Socrates, and the pre-Socratics, Gilson's humanism emphasizes the centrality of the human person, the subjects it studies that have a direct bearing on the centrality and dignity of the human person, and the way it studies these subjects increases the dignity of the philosophical act.

I call attention to this issue of Gilson's scholarly humanism for several reasons. One is that, despite its evident influence on Gilson's scholarship, his way of attacking philosophical problems, I do not think many Thomists have thought about it as a form of humanism. Another is that, while later twentieth-century and early twenty-first century scholars might have largely ignored this quality of Gilson's intellectual life, early twentieth-century thinkers would likely have found it glaring, so glaring that they might have found Gilson suspect because of it.

A brief review of Gilson's educational background gives insight into why a general interest in classical studies: (1) should have been a main influence in the way Gilson approached scholarship and (2) would provide for him the wider context within which to make intelligible the thought of others to himself and his audience. As described by Gilson's authoritative biographer Lawrence K. Shook (and as I have written about more extensively in my Chapter 1 of this collective volume), Gilson's formal education that took its start at home under the longdistance supervision of Ursiline sister Mother Saint-Dieudonne was immersed in the liberal arts. After this, in 1890, he entered the Christian Brothers' run parish school of Ste-Clotilde where, among other things, he received educational grounding in Latin, catechism, and love of language. In 1895, Gilson left Ste-Clotilde to start seven years of education at the Catholic secondary school, Petit Séminaire de Notre-Dame-des-Champs. There he underwent rigorous training in classical ("humanistic") studies that included ancient Greek, Latin, Roman and French history, mathematics, physical science, liturgy, and music.

Gilson left Notre-Dame-des-Champs in 1902 to attend a year of studies at the celebrated Lycée Henri IV. While there, Gilson was introduced to philosophy by Professor Henri Dereux and attended Lucien Lévy-Bruhl's course on David Hume. Gilson graduated from Lycée Henri IV in 1903 with a bachelor's diploma and certification from the Faculty of Letters at the University of Paris that would permit him to continue his studies at the Sorbonne.

Gilson enrolled in the Sorbonne in 1904 and completed his studies there in three years. Especially memorable to Gilson during this time were a course on Descartes he took under Lucien Lévy-Bruhl and a set of lectures that Henri Bergson gave at the Collège de France. Lévy-Bruhl's course so strongly influenced Gilson that he decided to write his doctoral thesis on Descartes under Lévy-Bruhl's direction. Other major thinkers with whom Gilson studied during this time included Émile Durkheim and Victor Delbos.

Jumping ahead from this period of formal education to that of teacher and public lecturer, as long ago as 1926, when he made his first visit to North America to participate in an international congress in Montreal on "Education and Citizenship," Gilson was bothered by the conviction that not enough good students existed at the time capable of doing advanced work in philosophy. In 1929, in part to help solve this problem, he established his Institute of Mediaeval Studies (later to become The Pontifical Institute of Mediaeval Studies [PIMS]) at the University of Toronto; but I think Gilson's interest in founding this famed Institute went deeper than this.

Throughout his adult intellectual life, Gilson was convinced that, during the later Middle Ages, under the influence chiefly of 'Latin Averroism,' Western culture had suffered a psychological rupture between faith and reason that has continued until modern times and has caused a political secularization of modern education and an increased propensity to engage in global war. In *Reason and Revelation in the Middle Ages*, he tells any historian who might investigate the sources of 'modern rationalism' that an uninterrupted chain of influence exists from the Averroistic tradition of the Masters of Arts of Paris to the European freethinkers of the seventeenth and eighteenth centuries (the so-called 'Age of Reason').

Accompanying this fracture across the centuries, there arose, Gilson thought, an ever-increasing loss of the sense of a classical Western, philosophically-based humanism rooted in what, in his book *The Unity of Philosophical Experience*, Gilson had called the "Western Creed." He was equally convinced that these problems could only be reversed by recovering a true Christian humanism in education. Without recovering an understanding of, and belief in, this Western Creed, Western culture, Gilson thought, would collapse.

In my opinion, as a result of his experiences during World War I and his research into the influence of Latin Averroism on the subsequent rupture between faith and reason at the tail end of the Middle Ages, part of the reason Gilson founded this Pontifical Institute was to counteract the growth of the influence on Western culture of what I have labeled "neo-Averroism"—the contemporary Western tendency to maintain the rupture between faith and reason that Latin Averroism had initiated. I maintain that Gilson thought he could best combat this mindset through a philosophically-based humanism that defended the Western Creed. Explicitly or not, Gilson established the Pontifical Institute, I think, as a kind of renaissance institute similar to that of Lorenzo Valla's Platonic Academy, with the express purpose of using medieval renaissance wisdom to counteract the secularization of the West under the centuries-old philosophical deconstruction initiated by the Italian renaissance and the neo-Averroism of the Enlightenment counter-renaissance.

In support of my claim, I refer to the fact that around mid-December, 1933, Gilson presented a series of three lectures on "Le société chrétienne universelle" at Salle Saint-Sulpice, Montreal. At this time, Gilson started to become convinced that, by decreeing faith and reason to be irreconcilable and by separating the political world into one empire directed by the pope and another by the prince, Latin Averroism had fractured the medieval Christian hope of a Christian social order rooted in moral law, justice, and charity.

Shortly after this, in 1934, under the influence of Fr. Phelan and Basilian Fr. Henry Carr, Gilson went to Rome with them to hold meetings with the Sacred Congregation of Seminaries and Universities to discuss a charter for the Institute. After these meetings, in late March of the same year, Jacques Maritain accompanied Gilson to a private audience with Pope Pius XI. This meeting put the request for a charter firmly on the Congregation's agenda. After a provisional refusal in 1936, final approval came on 21 November 1939.

Beyond this, in 1934, Gilson published *La théologie mystique de saint Bernard*. Also in 1934, in preparing a policy statement for another journal, *Sept*, which his friend Fr. Bernadot had just established, to unify French Catholics and reverse the French republic's educational program of secularization, Gilson repeated this theme of overcoming the political divorce between faith and reason. This policy statement then served as background for a collection of articles entitled "Pour un ordre catholique" that he published in *Sept* related to education and political and social problems.

Gilson's first article in this collection, "En marge de Chamfort," attacked French intellectuals for having formed their own secular priesthood for controlling politics. His second article was a review of G. K. Chesterton's biography of St. Thomas Aquinas, *St. Thomas Aquinas: The Dumb Ox*, in which Gilson marveled at Chesterton's ability to penetrate into the essence of Thomas's thought. According to Shook, reading Chesterton caused Gilson to realize that, just as Chesterton had seen English Protestant historians writing history backwards, from the perspective of their understanding of the Reformation, "Gilson now saw French historians writing it from the vantage point of seventeenth-century rationalism,"[2] or according to what, once again, I call "neo-Averroism."

I also refer to comments Shook makes about an article that Gilson had written shortly before the outbreak of World War II in 1939, "Erasme: citoyen du monde." Commenting on the article, Shook says that, at heart, Gilson was an Erasmian humanist "who wanted to end all wars and to liberate men to work out their salvation in the context of personal freedom. He believed that this could be achieved through the kind of education that fostered the acquisition of moral

---

[2] Lawrence K. Shook, *Étienne Gilson* (Toronto, Pontifical Institute of Mediaeval Studies, The Gilson Series 6, 1984), 218. Most of the preceding biographical information about Gilson is taken from Shook.

virtue through the writings of Cicero and Seneca, and through the teachings of Christ."[3]

According to Shook, during this period, Gilson's main motivation "was to drive home to his Institute students that in humanism lay the best antidote to the venom of war. For Gilson medieval universalism, or 'true humanism' as Maritain called it, held the key to the ultimate health in the human condition."[4]

Because Gilson thought that, to be of use, students needed to analyze Christian humanism philosophically, he thought he had to present humanism within the context of the lives of men who lived it, historical humanists, humanist intellectuals continuing a tradition of classical learning through a series of intellectual renaissances, the high point of which had been the Medieval Renaissance. Hence, in the fall, 1939, Shook says that, after publishing his monograph *Dante et la philosophie* (Paris), Gilson offered to his Toronto students a public course of twelve lectures on Roman Classical Culture from Cicero to Erasmus in which he led his students through the transmission of classical humanism to Christianity through a series of renaissances covering the eighth through the fifteenth centuries.

Shook states that as World War II came to an end, Gilson became increasingly devoted to realizing the possibility of that *ordre catholique* he had advocated in the 1930s. He was convinced that German Hitlerism, Russian communism, Italian and Spanish fascism and American Deweyism had stood in the way then: each of them had focused on the production of their own brand of citizen,

---

[3] Shook, *Étienne Gilson*, 254.

[4] Shook, *Étienne Gilson*, 239.

and none of them had seen a pressing need for the teaching of moral and intellectual virtue. Now… real changes were finally possible.[5]

To address these changes, in 1945, Gilson wrote an article for *Le monde* entitled "Instruire ou éduquer?" in which he argued for the need to: (1) have greater concern for students as individuals, not prospective adherents to a political cause, and (2) familiarize students from infancy with moral virtues of the individual such as honor, duty, justice, and piety.

He quickly followed this article with four others that had the same keynote theme: The first step of any totalitarian regime is to seize the schools in order to have exclusive monopoly over shaping tomorrow's citizens.[6] In these articles, Gilson sought to focus educators' attention on inculcating personal virtue, not the power of movements. He entitled them: (1) "Hitler fera-t-il notre revolution?"; (2)" La circulaire 45 ou: comment l'on se propose de pervertir la vérité"; (3) "La revolution ou l'amitié redressera la Cité"; and (4) "La schisme national."

He published the articles in Stanislas Fumet's religiously-oriented journal *Hebdomadaire du temps present*. About a month after publishing these articles, Gilson published "Pour une education nationale" in *La vie intellectuelle*. He argued therein that free education must include religion. In another article published around this same time in *La croix*, entitled "La liberté de l'enseignement en Angleterre," Gilson expressed his admiration for the open British conformist and non-conformist educational policy in contrast to France's closed State-controlled one.

---

[5] Shook, *Étienne Gilson*, 254.

[6] Shook, *Étienne Gilson*, 254.

On 15 March 1945, he spoke before a packed meeting of *La Jeunesse Intellectuelle* in *La Grande Salle de la Mutualité*. As a result of these educational works, Gilson started to correspond with many of the leading intellectuals in post-liberation France and to become recognized as a spokesman for them. As a result, the French Ministry of Foreign Affairs selected him to join his friend Jacques Maritain as part of the French delegation to the 1945 San Francisco meeting to plan the United Nations charter, which was signed on 26 June of that year.

After returning to Toronto for a few months in anticipation of teaching his fall courses, Gilson was informed that the French Foreign Ministry had named him to as a participant in the October and November 1945 London conference designed to create the constitution for what would later become UNESCO, the United Nations Educational, Scientific, and Cultural Organization. Gilson served on the committee that drafted UNESCO's constitution.

During his stay in London, Gilson wrote five articles about the conference that were published in *Le monde*. Several others appeared over the next several years. In them, among other things, Gilson expressed his disappointment about the limited roles intellectuals would actually have in UNESCO. He also later expressed disappointment about the behavior of intellectuals at UNESCO's first general conference in Paris in 1946. In a radio discussion in which he took part with several other conference participants after the meeting regarding the question "Can UNESCO Educate for World Understanding?", Gilson maintained that the world would not be ready for global understanding until university education became more international than it then was. I think this is something Gilson hoped to achieve through his Toronto Institute.

While many people would call Gilson a neo-scholastic, Gilson considered himself to be chiefly a Christian humanist and his Thomism to be a Thomist humanism. He thought that the Christian-inspired humanism of classical Western culture embodied in the Western Creed rooted in classical philosophical realism was the best antidote for the ills of the contemporary world. Hence, he sought to imbue all his scholarly work, including his famed Pontifical Institute of Mediaeval Studies, with this humanism.

On 22 March 2011, the Vatican issued a declaration entitled *Decree on the Reform of Ecclesiastical Studies of Philosophy*, regarding the crucial role of philosophy, especially metaphysics, in training priests. Commenting upon this declaration, Vatican Secretary of Education Cardinal Zenon Grocholewski said that the most fundamental aspects of life are under assault today: "[R]eason itself is menaced by utilitarianism, skepticism, relativism and distrust of reason's ability to know the truth regarding the fundamental problems of life."[7] He added that "science and technology, those icons of what he called materialist philosophies, cannot satiate man's thirst in regard to the ultimate questions: What does happiness consist of? Who am I? Is the world the fruit of chance? What is my destiny? etc. Today, more than ever, the sciences are in need of wisdom."[8] The Cardinal added that the study of philosophy must be returned to its

---

[7] Cardinal Zenon Grocholewski, "Vatican: Priests Can't Skip Metaphysics," ZENIT (22.03.2011), http://www.zenit.org/article-32095?l= english, access: July 16, 2012.

[8] Grocholewski, "Vatican: Priests Can't Skip Metaphysics."

roots in reason, adding that, because of the present crisis of Christian culture, logic, the discipline that gives structure to reason, has "disappeared."[9]

I think Gilson would largely concur with the Vatican declaration and the statements of Cardinal Grocholewski. But I think he would add that what they propose is not enough. Beyond this return to the study of philosophy and metaphysics, and recovery of the study of logic, I suspect Gilson would maintain, with me, that the West needs that new humanism about which Pope Benedict spoke in his encyclical *Caritas in veritate*. In returning to philosophy and metaphysics, the West does not need to return to Cartesian-Thomism and to a wisdom that mistakes philosophy for systematic logic. It needs a philosophy, a metaphysics, rooted in sense realism and faculties of the human person—a new humanism that can properly identify and resolve the fracture between faith and reason initiated by Latin Averroism. And it needs an intellectual academy, a circle of scholars, capable of training students to understand and defend their own intellectual tradition, the Western Creed. *In short, the West and the world needs Gilsonian humanism and a flourishing International Étienne Gilson Society*!

[9] Grocholewski, "Vatican: Priests Can't Skip Metaphysics."

Chapter 4

Standing on the Shoulders of Giants to Refine Gilson's Teaching about Christian Philosophy[1]

Introduction: Generic Definition of Philosophy as an Individual and Cultural Enterprise

As the title of my paper suggests, so as to make it more precisely intelligible, my chief aim in this presentation is to call upon the research of some exceptional scholars to make some refinements to Étienne Gilson's teaching about the nature of Christian philosophy. The first of these scholars, or intellectual giants, is the great American educator, and Gilson's friend, Mortimer J. Adler and two statements he noted Aristotle had made about investigation of truth as, always and everywhere, a culturally- and individually-generated

[1] The following historic article is an expanded revision of a Plenary Session paper I presented as part of the 150th Anniversary Celebration of the Founding of École Pratique des Hautes Études in Paris, France, The Sorbonne (Liard Amphitheater)—a Special EPHE-Sponsored International Colloquium on "Étienne Gilson (1884–1978), Medievalist and Philosopher, Man of Faith and Man of Action," which, at his request, I co-organized with Michel Cacouros, EPHE Maître de conférences Habilité, Sciences Historiques et Philologique, 20 September 2018. I am honored to have *Studia Gilsoniana* now publish it. I thank the current editor-in-chief of *Studia Gilsoniana*, Imelda Chłodna-Błach for granting me permission to republish it here in its slightly revised form.

"doable human deed"[2]: 1) "The investigation of the truth is, in one way hard, in another easy. An indication of this is found in the fact that no one is able to attain the truth adequately, while, on the other hand, we do not collectively fail, but everyone says something true about the nature of things, and, while individually we contribute little or nothing to the truth, by the union of all a considerable amount is amassed."[3] 2) "It is necessary ... to call into council the views of those of our predecessors ... in order that we may profit by whatever is sound in their suggestions and avoid their errors."[4]

At least by implication, Adler understood Aristotle to be saying that, by nature, in its generic definition, philosophy is chiefly a co-operative-and-transgenerational, individual and cultural, psychological enterprise (or a transgenerational, organizational, psychological habit: a co-operative individual and cultural historical habit of an individual human soul and, analogously considered, a cultural, educational one). In understanding philosophy in this way, Adler would have recognized himself to be agreeing with St. Bernard of Chartres that philosophy is a cultural enterprise in which, to enter, and progress, "like dwarfs," we need to "stand on the shoulders of

[2] Mortimer J. Adler, "Philosophy's Past, Present, and Future," in *The Great Ideas Online*, 899 (January 2017), 6. For a more detailed discussion of this topic, see Adler, *The Four Dimensions of Philosophy*: *Metaphysical, Moral, Objective, Categorical* (New York: Macmillan, 1993).

[3] Aristotle, *Metaphysics*, trans. W. D. Ross, in Richard Mc Keon (ed.), *The Basic Works of Aristotle* (New York: Random House, 1941), Bk. 2, ch., 1, 993b1–993b4. Cited after Adler.

[4] Aristotle, *On the Soul*, Bk. 1, ch. 2, trans. J. A. Smith, in Mc Keon (ed.), *The Basic Works of Aristotle*, 404a20–23. Cited after Adler.

giants" (a statement historically attributed to Bernard by John of Salisbury).[5]

Evident from what Aristotle and Adler had said above is that both had considered history to be a philosophical laboratory, or *testing ground*, that measures philosophically-doable deeds, or exercise of philosophy. Evident from Gilson's periodic use of the term 'enterprise' generically to define philosophical activity and of history as a laboratory measure of truth of philosophical claims is that: 1) he had strongly concurred with Adler on this point; and 2) he had done to such an extent that he had considered historically testing philosophical (that is, psychological) claims (that is, assertions made through a human soul) to be a first principle for recognizing cultural exercise of philosophy!

Were this not the case, how do we explain the nature of Gilson's masterful monograph, *The Unity of Philosophical Experience*? Within this work, after engaging in several failed historical experiments in which Gilson wonders how many such tests will have to be conducted "before men gain some philosophical experience," *like a good psychologist*, Gilson diagnosed the principal cause of contemporary Western philosophical disorders to be the psychological one of attempting to think and choose the way we wish instead of thinking and choosing the way we can.[6]

---

[5] Ralph M. McInerny, *A History of Western Philosophy*, vol. 2, *Philosophy from St. Augustine to Ockham* (University of Notre Dame Press: Notre Dame, Ind. and London, United Kingdom, 1970), 160.

[6] Étienne Gilson, *The Unity of Philosophical Experience* (New York: Charles Scribner's Sons, 1965, first published in 1937), 59. This work was reprinted by Ignatius Press (San Francisco, 1999), with a "Foreword" by

How, Early in the French Debates about Christian Philosophy, Gilson Adopted a Maritainian Distinction Historically to Apprehend Philosophically Doable Deeds

As Gilson tells us in his metaphysical/aesthetic masterpiece, *Painting and Reality*, we predicate the term 'possible' in two ways: in a first sense to refer to conceptual thinkability in which "we call possible whatever is not intrinsically impossible—that is, any object whose notion is not self-contradictory"; and, "in a second sense ... we call possible whatever, after being conceived by the mind, can be made to exist in reality": a really doable deed.[7]

While Gilson does not say so explicitly within the context of the passages cited in the text, the first understanding of 'possible' corresponds to an abstract psychological act: the abstract mode of speculative, conceptual consideration about essences in which Aristotelian logicians tend to engage. The second conforms to a concrete psychological act: the actual way of considering that human beings tend to use when thinking about alternative choices, such as whether or not to undertake a given action is a doable human deed. While, abstractly considered, a thing, or action, might be psychologically conceivable in principle and nature, concretely considered, and in actuality and strictly speaking, it might not be able to exist, or be

---

Desmond J. FitzGerald. See, also, Gilson's 1931–1932 University of Aberdeen Gifford Lectures (published in French as *L'esprit de la philosophie médiévale* ([Paris, J. Vrin, 1932] and in English as *The Spirit of Medieval Philosophy* [New York, Charles Scribner's Sons, 1932]).

[7] Étienne Gilson, *Painting and Reality*, vol. 4 of the A. W. Mellon Lectures in the Fine Arts (New York: Published for the Bollingen Foundation by Pantheon Books, vol. XXXV in the Bollingen Series, 1958), 158.

doable for anyone, or any culture or civilization, at anytime, anywhere (for example, strictly speaking, practice of Christian philosophy by an ancient, pagan Greek philosopher).

This distinction about two concepts of 'possible' is crucial to note because Gilson: 1) repeatedly uses it to weave together different scenarios within *The Unity of Philosophical Experience* to transform this work from a tale of disparate psychological experiments in philosophical activity into a powerful, organic, whole book in philosophical history; and 2) early in the Christian philosophy debates that had started in France during the first few decades of the twentieth century and later, Gilson would refer to this twofold distinction in terms initially coined by Jacques Maritain of the difference between the: 1) "order of specification"; and 2) "order of exercise."

In support of the first of the two claims that I have just made about these two different understandings of 'possible' (abstract and logical as opposed to concrete and real) and the way they refer to the orders of specification and exercise, consider what Gilson says about telling the historical tale of intellectual experiments that he had entitled *The Unity of Philosophical Experience*:

> The philosophical events which have been described in the previous chapters cannot be wholly understood in the sole light of biography, of literary history, or even of the history of the systems in which they can be observed. They point rather to the fact that, in each instance of philosophical thinking, both the philosopher and his particular doctrine are ruled from above by an impersonal necessity. In the first place, philosophers are free to lay down their own sets of

> principles, but once this is done, they no longer think the way they wish—they think the way they can. In the second place, it seems to result from the facts under discussion, that any attempt on the part of a philosopher to shun the consequences of his own position is doomed to failure. What he himself declines to say will be said by his disciples, if he has any; if he has none, it may eternally remain unsaid, but it is there, and anybody going back to the same principles, be it several centuries later, will have to face the same conclusions. It seems, therefore, that though philosophical ideas can never be found separate from philosophers and their philosophies, they are, to some extent, independent of philosophers and well as of their philosophies, taken in their naked, impersonal necessity of both their contents and their relations. The history of these concepts and their relationships is the history of philosophy itself. Philosophy consists in the concepts of philosophers, taken in their naked impersonal necessity of both their contents and their relations. The history of these concepts and their relations is the history of philosophy itself.[8]

As far as my second claim (that Gilson would refer to this twofold distinction in terms coined by Maritain of the difference between the: 1) "order of specification"; and 2) "order of exercise"), in his *An Essay on Christian Philosophy*, Maritain directly quotes Gilson's *Spirit of Medieval Philosophy* as agreeing with Maritain on this point:

[8] Gilson, *The Unity of Philosophical Experience*, 301–302.

Consider any given philosophic system. Now ask if it is 'Christian,' and if so by what characteristics you can recognize it as such? From the observer's standpoint it is a philosophy, therefore a work of reason. The author is a Christian and yet his Christianity, however telling its influence on his philosophy has been, remains essentially distinct from it. The only means at our disposal for detecting this inner action is to compare this data which we can outwardly observe. The philosophy without revelation and the philosophy with revelation. This is what I have attempted to do. And since history alone is capable of performing this task, I have stated that history alone can give meaning to the concept of Christian philosophy.... I may say, then, that Christian philosophy is an objectively observable reality for history alone, but that once its existence has been thus established, its notion may be analyzed in itself. This ought to be done as Mr. J. Maritain has done it; I am in fact in complete agreement with him.[9]

---

[9] Jacques Maritain, *An Essay on Christian Philosophy*, trans. Edward H. Flannery (New York: Philosophical Library, 1955), x, n. 1.

Some Observations and Claims about Principles Gilson had Used Historically to Test Philosophical Activity

Most striking to me about the different historical reoccurrences of philosophical inexperience that Gilson recounts in his philosophical thriller, *The Unity of Philosophical Experience*, is: 1) Gilson's own many failed attempts over several decades precisely to explain the meaning of 'Christian philosophy' to himself and to others; and 2) what chiefly caused these failed attempts to happen.

As a case in point, moving on to consider the first of several observations and claims about principles Gilson had used historically to test philosophical activity, Gilson had firmly accepted Aristotle's claim that small mistakes made about first principles in the beginning of an investigation tend to multiply many times as the study continues.[10] A chief reason I say Gilson had firmly accepted this claim is because he repeatedly applies this principle in his *The Unity of Philosophical Experience* as his historical laboratory-measure of philosophical legitimacy.

A second striking case in point striking about the different historical reoccurrences of philosophical inexperience that Gilson recounts in this work are some similarities and differences between them and several other historical events: 1) Gilson's many failed attempts over several decades precisely to explain the meaning of 'Christian philosophy' and the many incarnations his definition underwent; 2) what chiefly caused these failed attempts to happen; 3) how Gilson reacted to these failures; and 4) something crucial we

[10] Aristotle, *On the Heavens*, trans. J. L. Stocks, in Mc Keon (ed.), *The Basic Works of Aristotle*, Bk. 5, Ch. 1, 271b 9–10.

can learn from his philosophical failures about the nature of philosophical, scientific, failure in general.

Some Chief Causes for Gilson's Many Failed Attempts Precisely to Explain the Meaning of 'Christian Philosophy' to Himself and to Others

As anyone who has studied Gilson's many tries to explain the meaning of 'Christian philosophy' knows, his understanding of Christian philosophy underwent several incarnations. This started on 21 March 1931 when, at a meeting of the Société française de philosophie, he and Jacques Maritain had attempted to defend the notion of a Christian philosophy in response to a 1928 article by Émile Bréhier's in which, historically considered, Bréhier had denied its existence.[11] This debate lasted until at least as late as Gilson's 1962 monograph, *The Philosopher and Theology.*

In my opinion, as unbelievable as the following claim might sound, the chief reason for these many failed attempts is that, like all the other leading figures involved in this debate from the start, and like the many intellectuals he had criticized through his psychological/philosophical analysis, Gilson had begun his research short on philosophical experience: he and those debating with him had not adequately comprehended how Aristotle and St. Thomas had understood, precisely defined, 'philosophy.' Not having grasped this, the different participants in the debate then claimed to see, or not

[11] Émile Bréhier, "Y-a-t-il une philosophie chrétienne," in *Bulletin de la Société française de philosophie*, 31, no. 2 (1931).

see, philosophy, and Christian philosophy, to exist, or not exist, within Western intellectual history.

For example, well-known is that Gilson had assumed something he had called 'philosophy' had historically transitioned as a cultural enterprise from the tail end of ancient Greek culture to medieval Christian culture. His whole laboratory method of testing for philosophy's existence depended upon the historical transitioning of this philosophical enterprise. As Gilson had understood the historical situation, strictly speaking, ancient Greeks had originated philosophy and medieval Christian culture had inherited what the Greeks had originated. In actuality, no such transitioning had actually taken place. As I have shown in my *Wisdom*'s *Odyssey from Philosophy to Transcendental Sophistry*, before the advent of Christianity, the ancient Greeks had largely lost their understanding of philosophy as thinkers like Socrates, Plato, and Aristotle had understood it. And the early Church Fathers were not chiefly interested in understanding the nature of the Greek philosophical enterprise considered as such; they were chiefly interested in it for apologetical reasons. Until St. Albert the Great and St. Thomas came on the scene, Catholic intellectuals had generally mistaken philosophy to be one or more of the liberal arts—something they continue to do to this day![12]

In addition, when Gilson had written *The Unity of Philosophical Experience*, he had defined precisely and abstractly what Christian

[12] For an extensive defense of this claim, see Peter A. Redpath, *Wisdom's Odyssey from Philosophy to Transcendental Sophistry* (Amsterdam and Atlanta: Editions Rodopi, B.V., 1997).

culture had inherited from the ancient Greeks, especially from Aristotle, as follows: "Philosophy consists in the concepts of philosophers, taken in their naked impersonal necessity of both their contents and their relations." While he had admitted that "philosophical ideas can never be found separate from philosophers and their philosophies" (that is, from existence within a human soul), he had immediately followed this admission with the statement that "to some extent these ideas are independent of philosophers and as well as of their philosophies, taken in their naked, impersonal necessity of both their contents and their relations." In so doing, he was making clear that he was predicating the term 'philosophy' analogously; and when he followed with a specific definition of philosophy, he was making equally clear that, no matter where it existed, he had considered philosophy to be chiefly a logical system of abstract essences, or ideas, and their impersonal, essential relations (not chiefly a psychologically doable deed, not chiefly an act of the human soul, or better, the human person).

Furthermore, he was making explicit, "The history of these concepts and their relationships is the history of philosophy itself." In other words, Gilson was saying that, once a person knowledgeable about philosophy's nature sees such a systematic body of knowledge, system of ideas, or set of logical premises existing within history, that person is experiencing philosophical exercise, and philosophical history in the making. He or she is not experiencing philosophy as a pure nature, or abstract essence specified by its abstract essence. He or she is experiencing philosophy being exercised in a specific state, specified by its existential state. Because that which is really actual must be really possible, Gilson saw such experience to be historical evidence of philosophy's possible state, its possible existence in a soul, be that soul Christian or pagan.

Considered in the way Gilson had described it, philosophy's pure nature resembles—as Gilson's colleague Anton C. Pegis had once referred to it— "some sort of an Avicennian absolute essence," existing somewhere apart from the human soul (by virtue, I would add, of its own *esse essentiae*, in a kind of essentialistic limbo, until it eventually re-enters the world of existence [*esse existentiae*] through exercise within a human soul).[13]

Quite striking to me about the way Gilson had defined 'philosophy' in 1937 is how un-Aristotelian, un-Thomistic, idealistic, essentialistic, and logicistic it was and sounds; and what is ironic and paradoxical about the way Gilson had defined this term in this monograph is that the first failed-experiment he mentions in the *The Unity of Philosophical Experience* he entitles "Logicism"! Especially ironic and paradoxical, about his doing this is that, shortly after writing this work (1937), in 1939, Gilson had published another work, entitled *Thomist Realism and the Critique of Knowledge*, in which he had claimed, in a much more personalistic and realistic tone, that sense apprehension of the being of singular natures is the first principle of all knowledge, including philosophical knowledge. Considered as such, it is more proximate in nature to philosophical reasoning than the logical principle of non-contradiction, which is a first principle of all logical reasoning, but not of all knowing.

---

[13] Anton C. Pegis, "*Sub Ratione Dei:* A Reply to Professor Anderson," in *New Scholasticism*, 39 (1965), 154.

In the process of drawing this conclusion, Gilson had paid special attention to the fact that apprehension of sensible being essentially involves a conjunction of two knowing faculties: universal and particular, or cogitative, reason (*ratio particularis*, or *cogitativa*), which, in human beings, is analogous to the estimative sense (instinct) in brute animals.[14] Following St. Thomas, Gilson had maintained that neither the human intellect nor the senses immediately knows the existence or nature of sensible beings. Instead, the individual person grasps these through a conjunction of universal and particular reason.[15]

A chief cause of all Gilson's subsequent, decades-long failures to adequately explain the nature of Christian philosophy to himself and to others, then, appears to me to have been threefold. When first entering this debate: 1) Gilson had misrepresented to himself philosophy as applied by the ancient Greeks chiefly to have been a logical system of ideas, an abstract essence specified as being philosophical by being systematically logical, purely rational (having no conceptual contradictions; for example, not mixing premises of faith

---

[14] Étienne Gilson, *Thomist Realism and the Critique of Knowledge*, trans. Mark A. Wauck (San Francisco: Ignatius Press, 1986), 197; initially published in French in 1939 by Librairie Philosophique J. Vrin under the title *Réalisme thomiste et critique de la connaissance*.

[15] *Summa theologiae, Sancti Thomae Aquinatis Doctoris Angelici. Opera Omnia*. Iussu Leonis XIII, Rome: Vatican Polyglot Press, 1882–, 1, q. 78, a. 4; *On Truth*, trans. Robert W. Mulligan, J. V. McGlynn, and R. W. Schmidt (3 vols., Chicago: Henry Regnery Company, 1952–1954), q. 2, a. 6, ad 3; *Commentary on the Nicomachean Ethics of Aristotle*, Bk. 6, lect. 1, nn. 1118 and 1123; lect. 9, nn. 1249 and 1254–1255; *A Commentary on Aristotle's De anima*, trans. Robert Pasnau (New Haven, Conn. and London: Yale University Press, 1999), Bk. 3, lect. 745.

and reason); 2) he had accepted and applied Maritain's mistaken understanding of specification by abstract, or pure, essence as an act distinct from, and, in a way, capable of being intelligible without prior reference to specification by exercise; and 3) he appears not explicitly to have realized that, according to Aristotle and St. Thomas, all specification of human activity first exists in the human soul in an order of psychological exercise (a doable deed) in relation to a formal object related to a faculty or habit of the human soul! After so existing, it may then be psychologically transferred by logicians to abstract conceptual consideration of an essence, or definition, without actual and explicit reference to concrete exercise.

In short, despite the fact that, at least by 1939, Gilson appears to have been explicitly aware of the distinction I am presently making, he appears to have temporarily forgotten that the abstract, logical act of conceptualization and the concrete act of philosophical specification are generically different psychological acts, personal acts involving a human soul as their proximate generator.

Special note should be made here that in this case, contrary to the many philosophical failures he had examined in his *The Unity of Philosophical Experience*, Gilson did not blame his defeats on philosophy. Like Socrates, he blamed them on himself. This is a lesson in philosophical experience that Gilson had considered crucial for all aspiring philosophers to learn. Like any good researcher, scientist, Gilson had realized that philosophical failure is an essential part of specifying a generic nature.

By so behaving, through many small failures, progressively over several decades, he was able to jettison his mistaken definition of philosophy's nature as chiefly a system of logical premises, or body of knowledge (or habit of the soul whose formal object is a system of logical premises, or body of knowledge) and more precisely come close properly to specifying its definition as a psychological habit whose genus is not the same as the genus of the logician. Still, from 1939 onward, had he followed the understanding of philosophy that he had started to articulate in *Thomist Realism and the Critique of Knowledge*, instead of the one he had expressed his *The Unity of Philosophical Experience*, he could have improved his understanding of Christian philosophy much sooner, with even fewer failures.

How the Research of Armand A. Maurer Helps Serve as a Midwife to Give Birth to the Fully-Formed Nature of Christian Philosophy

Four years before Gilson's death in 1978, one of his two most-famous students, Armand A. Maurer (the other being Joseph Owens) contributed a much, since then, under-read and under-appreciated article entitled, "The Unity of a Science: St. Thomas and the Nominalists."[16] Had Gilson read this article about fifty years prior to

[16] Armand A. Maurer, "The Unity of a Science: St. Thomas and the Nominalists," in *St. Thomas Aquinas 1274–1974 Commemorative Studies*, vol. 2. Ed.-in-chief, Armand A. Maurer (Toronto: Pontifical Institute of Mediaeval Studies: 1974.) See, also, Maurer (trans.), *St. Thomas Aquinas, The Divisions and Methods of the Sciences, Questions V and VI of his Commentary on the de Trinitate of Boethius* (4th rev. edition, vol. 3, St Michael's College Mediaeval Studies in Translation, Toronto: Pontifical Institute of Mediaeval Studies,1986), 75, fns. 14 and 15. See, St. Thomas Aquinas, *The Sentences—Book 1: The Mystery of the Trinity*, trans. Giulio Silano (vol. 42, St Michael's College Mediaeval Studies in Translation, Pontifical Institute of Mediaeval Studies, 2007), Bk. 1, d. 19, q. 5, a. 2, ad 1; *Commentary on*

when Maurer had written it, I suspect he would have changed his tactical plan for explaining to himself and to others the nature of Christian philosophy.

Likely, what would have jumped out to him from this article would have been two claims by Maurer: that St. Thomas had understood 1) the genus, or subject, of the philosopher to be essentially different from the genus of the logician; and 2) philosophy to be chiefly a psychological habit (a habit of the human soul), not a body, or system, of knowledge; and only secondarily, analogously, to be a logical system, or body of knowledge. While he did not say so explicitly at the time, strictly speaking, what Maurer was maintaining about philosophy's genus was the *contrary opposite* of what, for decades, Gilson and Maritain would early on report and emphasize about it in relation to Christian philosophy as a historically observable nature. Having corresponded with Maurer at this time and until the end of his life, I am convinced he had never explicitly recognized this implication regarding Gilson's and Maritain's teaching regarding Christian philosophy.

According to Maurer, the conception of philosophy as chiefly a system or body of knowledge had originated with William of Ockham and his nominalistic followers, not with St. Thomas Aquinas. He called Ockham "its theoretician and popularizer."[17] In opposition to the Ockhamist understanding of philosophy, Maurer rightly claimed that St. Thomas had maintained all philosophy, science, to

---

the Metaphysics of Aristotle, Bk. 5, lect. 22, nn. 1121–1144; Bk. 10, lect. 12, nn. 2142–2144; and *Summa theologiae*, 1, q. 66, a. 2, ad 2 and 88, 2, ad 4.

[17] Maurer, "The Unity of a Science: St. Thomas and the Nominalists," 271.

be chiefly a habit of the soul (a psychological habit) that studies a real genus. A real, philosophical, or scientific, genus, in turn, he noted, consists in some really existing proximate subject abstractly-considered as a generator, proximate cause, of essential accidents (properties).

For example, as Fr. Charles Bonaventure Crowley notes, as an essential accident, or property, that a material form requires to have to be able to cause a limited action and, thereby, be complete as a substance, the substantial body generates: 1) dimensive limits to itself as a material substance (that is, it generates a material surface, or figured material, surface-boundary, which serves as the three-dimensional, proximate subject in which really different figures can exist as properties, or essential accidents, creating material boundaries for a substantial body; the substantial body the geometrician studies); and 2) within and through the surface body it has generated, it subsequently generates all qualitative properties that exist in that surface body (such as living organs in a living body) through which a substance, through the internal faculties it generates, is enabled to generate external acts (whose qualitative actions the physicist studies).[18]

Maurer had noted that this understanding of a genus essentially differs from that of the logician, which, for example, abstractly and univocally signifies the essence of a species (like animal being the

---

[18] Peter A. Redpath, "Editor's Prescript," in Charles B. Crowley, *Aristotelian-Thomistic Philosophy of Measure and the International System of Units (SI): Correlation of the International System of Units with the Philosophy of Aristotle and St. Thomas*, ed. with a prescript by Peter A. Redpath (Lanham, Md., New York, and London, United Kingdom: University Press of America, 1996), xii–xviii.

genus of man). Instead, the philosophical genus is the proper subject of different species of accidents (essential accidents, properties, like quantity and quality) and cannot properly be conceived apart from considering: 1) the way it exists and 2) its essential relation to the human soul as numerically-one habit within the soul.

If, analogously, we apply Maurer's claim about the existence of these two essentially different kinds of genera (logical and philosophical) as measures of what Maritain and Gilson had repeatedly said until late in their lives regarding the natures of philosophy and Christian philosophy as historically-observable realities, reasonable to conclude is that, at least by implication of his principles, when they talked about philosophy and Christian philosophy, Maurer would be accusing Maritain and Gilson of reporting an analogous and secondary, nominalistic, understanding of philosophy and Christian philosophy.

Opposed to this analogous understanding, Maurer had claimed St. Thomas had maintained, "Each of the speculative sciences has its own generic subject, or formal object, conceived through its unique mode of abstraction. Each science also has its own principles and mode of procedure, which produce in the intellect a habitus distinct from that of every other philosophy."[19] Considered as such, Maurer added, a science is numerically one habit of the soul (a psychological habit!) generated by repeated acts of a formal object, or subject genus, on the habit![20]

---

[19] Maurer, "The Unity of a Science: St. Thomas and the Nominalists," 291.

[20] Maurer, "The Unity of a Science: St. Thomas and the Nominalists," 271–274.

That is, essentially considered, Maurer was saying that St. Thomas had: 1) generically considered philosophy, science, to be chiefly a psychological habit whose formal object, or subject (external stimulus), is always some abstractly considered, composite, organizational whole; and 2) specifically considered divisions within this philosophical, or scientific, genus, to be psychological habits whose formal object, subject, is also always some abstractly considered, composite, organizational whole—philosophically, or scientifically, differentiated by the chief habitual interest, *ratio* ('notion,' 'way of thinking about'), or aim, in relation to which it intellectually considers the organizational whole it studies. For example, the sciences of biology and medicine are specifically differentiated as generic sciences of the human heart insofar as one (medicine) is habitually interested in and aims at studying the heart chiefly as health-generating while the other (biology) is habitually interested in and aims at studying the heart chiefly as life-generating.

Until the time of his death, I do not think Maurer ever fully comprehended that, based upon the way he was interpreting St. Thomas's teaching about philosophy, he had issued in a radically new understanding of philosophy as an organizational psychology. As a habit of the soul, philosophy is essentially a psychology. As a habit whose formal object is a generic organization of species, philosophy is specified as an organizational psychology!

Concisely put, just like any human habit, Maurer was saying that specification of a philosophy, or science, is determined by a chief habitual interest in some qualitatively different act that some qualitatively different organizational whole proximately causes or generates. Real, generic habits are always specified by their acts. And their acts are always specified by their formal objects: external stimuli, or chief aims. (Hence, the generically common habit of athletics becomes specified as the athletic habit of tennis or golf by the qualitatively different ways human muscles are habituated to harmonize to generate different physical acts to achieve qualitatively different chief athletic aims.)

As is evident from what St. Thomas says toward the start of his *Summa theologiae* about the nature of the subject, or formal object, of a science, Maurer was right. There, St. Thomas states, "[T]he subject of a science is related to the science just as an object is related to a faculty or habit."[21] That is, the subject, or formal object, of a science considered as a psychological habit (*habitus*) relates to a scientific habit of the human soul just as an external stimulus, like a sound, relates to the faculty of hearing. Considered as such, it is the formal object, external stimulus, of a psychological habit, a habit of the human soul, which is generically different from the formal object of the psychological habits of logic and history!

In making this reference to Maurer, *in no way am I stating, implying, or insinuating that Maritain and Gilson did not understand that St. Thomas had maintained philosophy, science, to be numerically one psychological habit, a habit of the human soul.* Nevertheless, *I am explicitly maintaining that, in talking about philosophy and Christian philosophy, Maritain and Gilson had repeatedly failed to report, emphasize, what St. Thomas chiefly had meant by a philosophical, or scientific, genus.* I am asserting that, not only did Maritain and Gilson repeatedly not precisely report and emphasize what St.

[21] Aquinas, *Summa theologiae*, 1, q. 1, a. 7, respondeo: "[S]e habet subjectum ad scientiam sicut objectum ad potentiam vel habitum."

Thomas chiefly had meant by a philosophical, or scientific, genus, for decades they had tended to convolute his understanding, reverse it, and sublimate it to an analogous caricature in which philosophy's formal object was no longer an acting subject abstractly considered as an organizational whole, or real genus, generating, through the harmonious action of its internallyexisting specific parts, numerically one organizational action.

Instead, philosophy's, science's formal object, became a static body of knowledge, or system of logical premises. By so doing, they tended to reduce St. Thomas's dynamic and concrete understanding of philosophy as an organizational psychology of organizational operation, or habit of studying organizational operations, into a static caricature: contemplation of abstractly considered essences. Decades later, Gilson would indirectly lament what he and Maritain had been doing, somewhat unwittingly, at the time: "Generation after generation of Schoolmen have mistaken the order of concepts in the mind for the order of things in reality."[22]

In criticizing Maritain's report of the nature and state of philosophy with which Gilson had initially agreed, I am not denying as licit the distinction between "the order of specification" and "the order of exercise." Nor am I claiming that Maritain and Gilson were totally oblivious to philosophy's dynamic nature as I have just defined it. I admit the distinction and deny that Maritain had properly tended to report and emphasize it. I maintain that, always and eve-

[22] Étienne Gilson, "In Quest of Species," Armand A. Maurer (ed.), in *Three Quests for Philosophy* (Toronto: Pontifical Institute of Mediaeval Studies, The Étienne Gilson Series, 31, 2008), 62.

rywhere, specification of a real genus first occurs in the order of exercise. Once it exists there, logicians and others can analogously transpose it and think about in terms of an abstract essence.

Precisely because it is chiefly a habit of the rational soul of an individual person, philosophical nature is never, and can never be, specified as an absolute nature (like a Platonic form or Avicennian essence) existing apart from the human soul in some order of specification existing separate from the exercise of real, individual, human sense rationality. As proof of this claim, I call as my witness what St. Thomas says in his famous "Treatise on Man" of his *Summa theologiae* about the specification of human rationality wherein, to the possible shock to some readers, he locates the specific difference of our human rationality in a *per se* otherness within the sensitive, or animal, part of the intellectual soul, which is sometimes found with and sometimes without reason! As a quality essentially existing as an accidental property within human rationality, like human rationality, like all divisions of a really-existing genus, philosophical rationality must be specified as animal rationality within its really existing genus: the sense, or animal, part of the human soul.[23]

---

[23] Aquinas, *Summa theologiae*, 1, q. 77, a. 3 respondeo: "Sed tamen considerandum est quod ea quae sunt per accidens, non diversificant speciem. Quia enim coloratum accidit animali, non diversificantur species animalis per differentiam coloris, sed per differentiam eius quod per se accidit animali, per differentiam scilicet animae sensitivae, quae quandoque invenitur cum ratione, quandoque sine ratione. Unde rationale et irrationale sunt differentiae divisivae animalis, diversas eius species constituentes. Sic igitur non quaecumque diversitas obiectorum diversificat potentias animae; sed differentia eius ad quod per se potentia respicit."

I am explicitly maintaining that, in talking about philosophy and Christian philosophy, Maritain and Gilson had repeatedly failed to report what St. Thomas chiefly had meant by a philosophical, or scientific, genus. I am explicitly claiming that St. Thomas had understood philosophy chiefly to be a habit of the soul whose formal object is an abstractly considered real genus, or generically-conceived substance: what today we would call an "operational, or dynamic, organization," an organization abstractly considered as a proximate generator of action. Only secondarily, in an analogous sense, did he consider philosophy to be a "body of knowledge," "system of logical premises," or "systematic logic."[24]

While, to my knowledge, no other student of St. Thomas before me has ever maintained the following to be the case, what is crucial to understand about the real subject genus St. Thomas conceived as a division of philosophy to study is that it is one hierarchically ordered, composite whole comprised of many qualitatively unequal species ranging from most to least perfect in relation to possession of some chief mode of existing: *being one, and acting. Philosophy always studies the problem of the One and the Many in terms of part/whole relations.*

---

[24] Aquinas, Summa theologiae, 1, q. 77, a. 3 respondeo: "Sed tamen considerandum est quod ea quae sunt per accidens, non diversificant speciem. Quia enim coloratum accidit animali, non diversificantur species animalis per differentiam coloris, sed per differentiam eius quod per se accidit animali, per differentiam scilicet animae sensitivae, quae quandoque invenitur cum ratione, quandoque sine ratione. Unde rationale et irrationale sunt differentiae divisivae animalis, diversas eius species constituentes. Sic igitur non quaecumque diversitas obiectorum diversificat potentias animae; sed differentia eius ad quod per se potentia respicit."

The subject genus of a philosophy is an organizational, or ordered, whole divided by contrary opposites (many species) unequally, more or less perfectly, possessing some, one generic act. This generic act, moreover, exists within the species as a principle of unequal relation uniting them together to bring this generic act to unity and perfection as their numerically-one end! For example, 1) the one generic habit of medicine studies contrary opposites of the most and the least perfect possession of one subject genus, health (ranging in species [the many] from most perfect health to most diseased) with the chief aim of maintaining and perfecting bodily health and driving out bodily disease; 2) economics studies the contrary opposites of the most and the least perfect possession of wealth (maximally wealthy and maximally poor [the many]) for maintaining and perfecting economic wealth and driving out economic poverty; 3) ethics studies the contrary opposites of moral virtue and vice (the most and the least prudential acts of choice [the many]) for the chief aim of maintaining and perfecting prudent choice and driving out imprudent choice in the individual situation; and 4) politics studies the contrary opposites of peace and war (the most and least perfect acts of social, personal relations [the many]) for the chief aim of maintaining and perfecting peace and driving out conflict within a political community.

Given the glaring nature of St. Thomas's teaching about the subject of a science or a division of philosophy, someone might easily and reasonably wonder how a scholar as familiar with his works as Gilson could have for so long somewhat misrepresented St. Thomas's teaching about the natures of philosophy and Christian philosophy? Actually, I think Gilson always had at least a generic sense of this truth, and that what we first perceive are real genera and species—organizational wholes—not totally discrete individuals, or simply wholes unrelated to parts.

How else are we reasonably to account for the startling claims he makes in his 1972 lectures entitled "In Quest of Species" (later edited into a monograph by Maurer) in which, in answer to the question, "What do we perceive first: wholes or their parts?," Gilson states:

> Aristotle answers: neither, and I think he was right. 'What is plain and obvious to us, at first,' he says, 'is rather confused masses, the elements and principles of which become later known to us by analysis.' Remarkably enough, the Philosopher then adds that because it begins with the senses, knowledge must proceed from generalities to particulars, 'for it is a whole that is best known to sense perception, and a generality is a kind of whole, comprehending within it many things, like parts.' I said 'remarkably enough' because of the trite saying *sensus est particularius, intellectus est universalium*. We only perceive individuals, we only know universals, or, more correctly perhaps, individuals are objects of sense perception, universals are objects of intellectual cognition.[25]

Since the epistemological Gordian Knot Gilson was trying to untie was complicated, he continued his attempt to unravel it by noting an apparent contradiction related to it, which he immediately attempted to resolve. If we really do not see species, how do we account for the fact that we say things such as we see a horse, man, and

[25] Gilson, "In Quest of Species," 37–38.

so on? In the tradition of Aristotle and the Scholastics as he had understood them, Gilson answered:

> What I perceive by sense is in itself something particular, but my perception of it is something confused. By observing it more closely, and analyzing it, reason forms a clearer notion of it. Seen from a distance, what I see is some thing. If it gets nearer, I see an animal; still nearer, a man. Finally, I see John or Peter. In the end, I think I am perceiving by sense, not the sensible qualities of the object, but its very nature. Of course, that is largely an illusion; but there is some truth in it, and in his commentary on Aristotle's *De anima*, Thomas Aquinas says why that illusion is justified up to a point. Both the same man, the same soul, perceive by the senses and conceive by the intellect. One should not say that our senses perceive this and our intellect conceives that, but rather that men know by sense and intellect. The two modes of knowledge communicate in the unity of the knowing subject. In Thomas' own words, 'Taken at its summit, man's power of sensing somehow participates in understanding because in man sense is conjoined to intellect.' In short, because I know that what I am perceiving is a dog, I say I see a dog. In so doing, I merely say that I see what I know I am seeing.

While what Gilson says about the fact that we human beings actually perceive real genera and species is, in part, quite profound (so profound that I think it had influenced Fr. Maurer's article "The Unity of the Sciences: St. Thomas and the Nominalists" that he wrote a few years later), nonetheless, it could have been even more profound and precisely accurate had he considered what he was saying against the background footnote appearing on page twenty of his monograph *Painting and Reality*: "Order is the only kind of unity that multiplicity can receive."[26]

Had he done so—and had he added to that statement the observations that: 1) the only way a multiplicity can receive order is by becoming parts of an organizational whole, and 2) the only way a multiplicity can be transformed from a disparate multitude into parts of an organizational whole is through unequally and co-operatively-generating numerically one aim, or co-operative organizational act—I think he would have revised his analysis of what he had claimed Aristotle had given as an answer to the question, "What do we perceive first: wholes or their parts?"

For, in answer to this question, neither Aristotle nor St. Thomas would have replied, "Neither." They would have replied, "Both." As both had realized, along with Gilson, *what we first, and can only, perceive is an existing unity*. If something does not exist, if it does not possess the act of existing as an actual unity, or whole, we cannot know it. What we first, and always, perceive, and later wonder about as sensible, philosophical subjects, are acting subjects—numerically one organizational wholes: individually existing, operational organizations; qualitatively-different, acting organizations; numerically one organizational generators of action organizationally unified through unequal, and harmonious, relation to numerically one final act. In short, what we first, and always, perceive is a unity of order.

---

[26] Gilson, *Painting and Reality*, 20, fn. 17.

And ordered unity can only exist within a multitude of parts unequally contributing to generating numerically one organizational harmony through execution, exercise, of numerically one co-operative action.[27]

In perceiving this or that, in a confounded, or conflated, way, we are perceiving a harmoniously acting, composite-unity, qualitatively different from some other harmoniously acting composite-unity. We first perceive things by sensing a harmonious unity, order, within a multitude, of harmoniously ordered parts constituting an organizational whole.

Consequently, Gilson cannot possibly be correct when he says that, first, we confusedly perceive a sensory whole and, later, through intellectual analysis, we discover its principles. We sensibly induce the whole in and through simultaneously sensing and conceiving its principles as co-operative parts, sources, of a qualitatively different, real organizational unity: a real organizational harmony. We perceive the real, numerically one whole simultaneously in and through perceiving its real organizational principles of action.

Despite claims to the contrary, as Sir Francis Bacon had correctly realized centuries ago, and St. Thomas had recognized when talking about different species of psychological abstraction, induction is not chiefly an act of logic, and it does not start with a confused perception.[28] It is an intellectual/sensory act of perceiving a one in a many —confounding, not confusing, in a single perception, awareness of

[27] Gilson, *Painting and Reality*, 20, fn. 17

[28] Sir Francis Bacon, "Aphorisms," in *Novum organum*. https://oll.libertyfund.org/title/bacon-novum-organum (First published in London, England by Bonham Norton and John Bill, 1620), 14 and 82.

a qualitatively unique harmony existing within a multitude of essentially co-operating parts: an organizational whole operating within its parts to generate an organizational unity. Considered as such, it precedes reasoning, logic! Upon perceptual and conceptual induction of this harmonious unity, all species of philosophical, scientific, wonder essentially depend, as a *per se*, or *per aliud*, *notum*, principle of all subsequent philosophical, scientific, activity. Right reason starts with right induction!

Hence, my answer about how a scholar as familiar with his works as Gilson could have for so long somewhat misrepresented St. Thomas's teaching about the natures of philosophy and Christian philosophy is that, from the start of this debate, Maritain and Gilson had been considering the nature of philosophy chiefly from the perspective of historians and logicians, not from the perspective of historians and philosophers. The tactical plan they had chiefly chosen to use to demonstrate to their doubting audiences (largely consisting of nominalistic logicians) the reality of Christian philosophy was to adopt a method similar to archeologists and systematic, dialectical, logicians: To show them through the fossil records of a once-living species how a new species had appeared within Western and global cultural geography, surpassing in its archeological artifacts cultural remains of its parent species!

Furthermore, while Gilson had been certain that, as an essential principle of Western civilization and of what, in *The Unity of Philosophical Experience*, he had called the "Western Creed," philosophy had transitioned from ancient Greek culture to Christian culture, clearly from what he says from his earliest to his latest writings, *amazingly, he had never precisely understood what the ancient*

Greeks, including Aristotle, and St. Thomas had meant by a 'species,' nor precisely what is the nature of a real species in relation to a real genus.

Such being the case, he could never have properly grasped precisely what Aristotle and St. Thomas had understood by the nature of philosophy, or of Christian philosophy, if it has one. And, such being the case, we can more precisely understand the great contribution Maurer's research makes to resolving the debate about the possible and actual existence and nature of philosophy and Christian philosophy, and many other issues as well.

Reconsidering Christian Philosophy's Nature in Light of the Preceding Observations

Following Maurer's research, if we reconsider philosophy and Christian philosophy chiefly to be habits of the human soul, several conclusions become immediately evident: 1) The terms 'philosopher' and 'philosophy' are predicated analogously. Since people of all genera of religious and non-religious affiliations *habitually wonder about causes of organizational wholes, and organizational actions*, the term 'philosopher' and 'philosophy' are, in some way, licitly applicable to pagans, religious individuals, and a multitude of people in between these, such as secular, non-religious, theists and non-theists (someone like the young Mortimer Adler, for instance). 2) Since philosophy is a cultural enterprise, and since historical records indicate that the ancient Greeks first started to wonder about the causes of organizational wholes as part of a prudential cultural enterprise, in a way, strictly speaking, the terms 'philosopher' and 'philosophy' would appear to be chiefly applicable to them and to those coming after them *who have enough prudence* to apply philosophical activity essentially the way the great ancient Greek philosophers like Socrates, Plato, and Aristotle had done. Referring to all other wonderers, strictly speaking, these terms would appear to be properly applicable analogously.

Nonetheless, the way the ancient Greeks had philosophized was essentially limited by their understanding of the universe considered as a genus (which was the generic formal object, external stimulus, of the psychological habit of ancient Greek philosophy, science). By nature, this universe was composed partly of an everlasting material (spheres of the heavens and the Earth) that had no temporal beginning in the past and no temporal end in the future. Within its deterministic spheres of the heavens existed a multitude of gods capable of the most morally praiseworthy and shameful acts. These entities constantly traveled to Earth to interfere in human life and other earthly activities. Since these gods engaged in contradictory and, at times, morally shameful activities within the pre-philosophically-conceived ancient Greek universe, and since, within this mythopoietic universe, they were the proximate first principles of all specific and individual actions, from its start with Thales, by nature, the philosophical-cultural Greek enterprise of philosophizing consciously and explicitly sought no divine influence, no inspiration from the gods, nor from their inspired sons (the poets) on its specific and individual activity.

So conceived, this universe was an organizational whole comprised of everlasting specific parts, into which, strictly speaking, no new species, divine influence, inspiration, or providence could ever enter or exit. Since it was temporally everlasting by nature, the question of what caused this universe to exist or remain in existence (the question of the universe being created, or not created, ex nihilo) was eventually considered essentially unphilosophical, unscientific, a conceptual contradiction. And, since it was essentially uninspired and uninspirable by the gods (who were increasingly [especially by Socrates, Plato, and Aristotle], philosophically, scientifically, reconceived to be uninterested in human affairs), the Christian notion of grace essentially entering into the ancient Greek philosophical and scientific universe was also philosophically and scientifically incoherent, an oxymoron.

Since all finite action in this universe was generated by specific individuals (individuals existing within species), the ancient Greek understanding of action essentially included no room for generic and specific progress. The Western idea of generic and specific novelty, progress in individual and organizational action (spontaneous generation of some specific and individual action that had never previously existed) was, in principle, essentially absent from it as a culturally prevailing and providential notion.

While such an idea might have been conceivable in principle and fact by someone (for example, by an atheist, or non-religious individual—someone like Aristotle), it never dominated to become an essential principle of the ancient Greek philosophical enterprise. Since their understanding of action was essentially flawed, so, too, was their understanding of conceptual and real, or behavioral, possibility and impossibility (contradiction and non-contradiction).

Moreover, also flawed was the ancient Greek understanding of human freedom, which, chiefly as a freely-doable deed the ancient

Greeks had never been able precisely to articulate (because they had not been able to adequately explain the nature of particular reason). Not even Aristotle had been able to fully give birth to the idea of an animal rationality proper to a free agent capable of exercising the philosophical, scientific, act of sense wonder.

Thus considered, it is reasonable to claim that, from start to end, the ancient Greek conception of philosophy and science was essentially flawed, only partially birthed. Since the conception of philosophy, science, was first adequately achieved in its nature by St. Thomas Aquinas (who claimed to be operating under the influence of divine grace and Christian theological cultural enterprise and teachings, including that about the immortality of the human soul in this life and the immortality of the human body in a heavenly afterlife), good reason exists to make two claims: 1) the proper genus of philosophical speculation is the Christian, not the ancient Greek, universe, and that the Christian philosophy, science, of St. Thomas gave birth to a concept of the human person from which the organizational psychology for generating philosophy, science, as a complete nature, or, at least, a more adequate notion of philosophy, science, than ancient Greek culture had been able to generate, could finally be realized; and 2) if this understanding of philosophy, science, is the proper, or more adequate than the ancient Greek, one, then it is reasonable to conclude that the proper way to predicate the terms 'philosopher,' 'philosophy,' 'science,' 'scientist,' is chiefly of the Christian philosophy of St. Thomas Aquinas and analogously of the philosophical enterprise practiced by the ancient Greeks and others to whom it might be somewhat applicable.

Chapter 5

Étienne Gilson as Philosophical Prophet: The Metaphysical Causes of Contemporary Terrorism, and How to Eradicate Them[1]

As the terrors and mass murders of the third millennium beset us daily on a global basis, prudence dictates that we seek help from people of wisdom of the past so that we might get as precise an understanding as possible of our current political situation and gain counsel from them about how we got into this trouble and sage advice about how we might best transcend it. Étienne Gilson's little known, but prophetic, opuscule, *The Terrors of the Year 2000*, written in 1948, and published by St. Michael's College of the University of Toronto, Canada, 1949, marks Gilson's reflections upon the devastations of the twentieth century and his sobering warnings about the future.[2] This is the sort of work to which people of prudence need to turn in this time of increasing international peril.

Gilson starts his reflections in this little work by noting how children of old "were taught to hold as certain that around the year One Thousand a great terror took possession of people." While scholars of his day made fun of this story, discounted it as legend, and said

---

[1] This is a slightly amended unpublished essay that I delivered at Paradise Valley Community College, Phoenix, AZ, USA, 02 May 2019.

[2] Étienne Gilson, *The Terrors of the Year 2000* (Toronto: St. Michael's College, 1949), 5. I thank my colleague at St. John's University, Richard Ingardia (r.i.p.), for first informing me about the existence of this work by Étienne Gilson.

they could find no evidence of the "so-called panic" that was "supposed to have paralyzed whole populations in the expectation of the approaching end of the world," Gilson says children of his time believed it, and "the really amazing thing" was that, as the *Chronicles* of the monk Raoul Glaber indicate, the story had some truth to it. For Glaber reports all sorts of wonders, including "a war, a pestilence, a famine, a fiery dragon and a whale the size of an island, marked the approach of the year 1000."

Approaching the year Two Thousand, Gilson contended human beings had witnessed far greater terrors, ones that would be a certainty for future historians even if those of the year One Thousand were not for historians of his day. Gilson then referred to the ravages of World War I, the millions of dead, his own vision of corpses of children in Ukranian villages and on the banks of the Volga; wandering "bands of children reduced to savagery, who later were to be mowed down with machine guns; and official documentation bearing witness to the fact that "parents devoured their children. Fathers and mothers like our own, like ourselves, but who knew the meaning of that frightful word: 'hunger.'"[3]

The Communist menace overtook Holy Russia and then threatened the entire world. The bloody armistice, misnamed "peace," followed from 1918 to World War II. China remained in a continual state of war. The "barbarous civil war" followed in "Most Christian Spain."

Then came the late 1930s and the German army hurling itself upon Europe for a second time, vanquishing, plundering, butcher-

[3] Gilson, *The Terrors of the Year 2000*, 5–7.

ing Poland, toppling Paris, and astonishing the world. Gilson maintains that Raoul Glaber's fiery dragons were nothing in contrast to the air bombardments that filled the skies of France, the South Sea Islands, China, Russia, Germany, Italy, and England and destroyed its once mighty navy. The atomic bombing of Hiroshima followed the genocidal holocaust against the Jews and led to a contemporary age in which the close of World War II yielded no lasting peace and gave birth to the dawn of a new era "where science, formerly our hope and our joy, would be the source of greatest terror."[4]

Within a few short pages, Gilson makes clear to his reader the nature of the terror he envisions besetting the Year Two Thousand. At the close of World War II, we human beings made our most astounding discovery, whose symbolism is more striking because it is involuntary: "the great secret that science has just wrested from matter is the secret of its destruction. To know today is synonymous with to destroy."

Gilson maintains that the discovery of nuclear fission goes far beyond being an inseparable union of good and evil involving: (1) "the most intimate revelation of the nature of the physical world," (2) "the freeing of the most powerful energy that has ever been held," and (3) "the most frightful agent of destruction which man has ever had at his disposal." He maintains, "The age of atomic physics will see the birth of a new world, as different from our own age as ours is from the world before steam and electricity." This new world presents the scientist with a tragic dilemma. We know so many things today that our science might preclude our ability to control our own

---

[4] Gilson, *The Terrors of the Year 2000*, 7.

domination. In former times, Gilson says, we human beings mastered nature by obeying her. From now on, he claims, we master nature by destroying her.[5]

Atomic physics is only the beginning. Succeeding the era of physics, Gilson predicts we will witness "the still more redoubtable one of biology." He says that very few laboratory workers of his day doubt "we are on the verge of a great mystery which may, any day, surrender its secret. We will be able to work, not only on inert matter, but even on life, and it is not only the breadth of our power but its very nature which will become terrifying; and the more so that here again, and for the same reason, the possibility of good is inseparable from that of evil."[6]

Gilson tells us that, during his time, the "horrible" and symbolic term, "Pasteurian arms," a reference to biological warfare, has become common. Gilson finds the term more impressive because it was the exact contrary to Pasteur's intention. Pasteur cultivated microbes "to attenuate the virulence of their cultures, and thus save human lives." He did not cultivate them, as some scientists did in Gilson's time and do today, to increase their virulence so as to kill, not cure. Given this new and destructive turn of science, Gilson predicts:

"The biology of tomorrow will allow more subtle, but not the less formidable, interventions in human destiny. Can we imagine the repercussions which the free determinations of the sexes will have some day, perhaps in the near future? Can we picture what would

[5] Gilson, *The Terrors of the Year 2000*, 7–9.

[6] Gilson, *The Terrors of the Year 2000*, 9.

happen in a world where we could not only turn out males and females at will, but select them and produce human beings adapted to various functions as do breeders with dogs or horses or cattle? In that future society which will know how to give itself slaves and even the reproducers which it needs, what will become of the liberty and dignity of the human person? For once, the most daring prophecies of H. G. Wells appear tame, for in *The Island of Dr. Moreau* they were still only working to transform wild brutes into men; in the future society, it is men whom they will be transforming into brutes—to use them to foster the ends of a humanity thenceforth unworthy of the name."[7]

Gilson maintains that these are no idle fears. The fears of the people of Raoul Glaber's time were restricted to a small part of the Earth. Today's terrors encompass the whole planet. And the people living around the year One Thousand knew what they feared, the time of tribulation prophetically announced in the *Apocalypse*, the time when, according to St. Irenaeus, the Antichrist will devastate all the Earth, which will precede "the end of the world when creation will have lasted six thousand years."[8]

Gilson is bemused by Irenaeus's reasoning. Irenaeus, he says, "knows so many things, that the future unfolds before him with all the regulated precision of a super-film." According to Irenaeus, the world will last exactly six thousand years because one day of creation equals a thousand years. "The answer is perfect!", Gilson quips.

But, wait. What if Irenaeus and Raoul Glaber got their mathematics wrong? Suppose that the six thousand years since the dawn

---

[7] Gilson, *The Terrors of the Year 2000*, 9–11.

[8] Gilson, *The Terrors of the Year 2000*, 11–13.

of creation did not come to an end around the year One Thousand. Suppose the Year Two Thousand were the more accurate date. At this point, Gilson says, "we stop smiling and an uncomfortable doubt slips into our mind." Especially so when we consider, "The scourges which have struck us, the menace of the blows which await us, do not favor abandoning this hypothesis. If the drama which we live does not announce the end of the world, it is a rather good dress rehearsal. Shall we see worse than Buchenwald, Lydice and Oradour-sur-Glane? Perhaps it is not impossible, but it is difficult to believe."[9]

At this point in his reflection, Gilson pauses anxiously, looks about, and asks, "But where is the Antichrist?" His answer, "Right there!" There he is: *Friedrich Nietzsche.*

A serious accusation. But is it justified? According to Nietzsche, yes. "*Ecce homo*, said Friedrich Nietzsche, of himself: behold the man!" (More precisely, in the section "Why I Write Such Excellent Books," Nietzsche calls himself "the *Antichrist.*" In the section, "Thoughts Out of Season," he calls himself "the first *Immoralist.*")[10] Does any man more deserve the title of *Antichrist* than he who brought Zarathustra's terrifying message to the modern world? Gilson thinks not. The message that Nietzsche murmurs to himself is the short sentence: "They do not know that God is dead." With Nietzsche, the transvaluation of values starts in earnest. Man wishes to make himself divine, usurp God's place, become God.

---

[9] Gilson, *The Terrors of the Year 2000*, 13–14.

[10] Friedrich Nietzsche, *The Philosophy of Nietzsche*, no editor or translator listed (New York: Random House, Modern Library, 1954), 858, 875.

According to Gilson, Nietzsche's demonic grandeur is that he knows what he is saying and doing. He knows that God is dead. For this reason, Gilson claims, Zarathustra's "name is *Ante-christus* as well as *Anti-christus*. 'Have you understood me?' he asks. Dionysus face to face with the Crucifix." He comes "*before*" and "*against*" Christ.

Gilson considers Nietzsche's declaration "the capital discovery of modern times." Compared to Nietzsche's discovery, Gilson maintains that, no matter how far back we trace human history, we "will find no upheaval to compare with this in the extent or in the depth of its cause." Clearly, Gilson thinks that Nietzsche's declaration of God's death signals a metaphysical revolution of the highest, widest, and deepest order. Nietzsche is metaphysical dynamite. He knows it, readily admits it. "This is not just our imagination," Gilson states. All we have to do is read Nietzsche's *Ecce Homo* to find proof that what Gilson says is true:

"I know my fate. A day will come when the remembrance of a fearful event will be fixed to my name, the remembrance of a unique crisis in the history of the earth, of the most profound clash of consciences, of a decree enacted against all that had been believed, enacted and sanctified right down to our days. I am not a man. I am dynamite."[11]

---

[11] Gilson, *The Terrors of the Year 2000*, 13–14. While Gilson gives no specific reference to the location of this and the ones that follow passages in Nietzsche's "*Ecce Homo*, this one starts the section "Why I am a Fatality." See "*Ecce Homo*," in *The Philosophy of Nietzsche*, 923–933.

Clearly, to Gilson, the terrors of the year Two Thousand are, in root cause, metaphysical. The chief clash of civilizations we face today is not between the politics of West and East, or the West and other political orders. It is a metaphysical clash between the ancient and modern West.

Gilson maintains that, from time immemorial, we in the West have based our cultural creed and scientific inspiration upon the conviction that gods, or a God, existed. All of our Western intellectual and cultural institutions have presupposed the existence of a God or gods. No longer. All of a sudden, God no longer exists. Worse: He never existed! The implication is clear: "We shall have to change completely our every thought, word and deed. The entire human order totters on its base."

If our entire cultural history depended upon the unswerving conviction that God exists, "the totality of the future must needs depend on the contrary certitude, that God does not exist." The metaphysical terror now becomes evident in its depths. Nietzsche's message is a metaphysical bomb more powerful than the atomic weapon dropped on Hiroshima: "Everything that was true from the beginning of the human race will suddenly become false." Moreover, mankind alone must create for itself a new self-definition, which will become human destiny, the human project.

What is that destiny, project? *To destroy.* Gilson tells us Nietzsche knows that, as long as we believe that what is dead is alive, we can never use our creative liberty. Nietzsche knows and readily admits his mission is to destroy. Hence, he says:

"When truth opens war on the age-old falsehood, we shall witness upheavals unheard of in the history of the world, earthquakes will twist the earth, the mountains and the valleys will be displaced, and everything hitherto imaginable will be surpassed. Politics will then be completely absorbed by the war of ideas and all the combinations of powers of the old society will be shattered since they are all built on falsehood: there will be wars such as the earth will never have seen before. It is only with me that great politics begin on the globe. . .. I know the intoxicating pleasure of destroying to a degree proportionate to my power of destruction."[12]

If Nietzsche speaks the truth about his project, which Gilson thinks he does, Gilson maintains the he is announcing the dawn of a new age in which the aim of postmodern culture, its metaphysical project, is to make war upon, to overthrow, traditional truths and values. To build our brave new world order, we have to overthrow the metaphysical foundations of Western culture. "Before stating what will be true, we will have to say that everything by which man has thus far lived, everything by which he still lives, is deception and trickery." As Nietzsche says, "He who would be a creator, both in good and evil, must first of all know how to destroy and to wreck values."

In fact, Gilson maintains, our traditional Western values are being wrecked all around us, everywhere, under our feet. He says he stopped counting "the unheard of theories thrown at us under names as various as their methods of thought, each the harbinger of a new truth which promises to create shortly, joyously busy preparing the brave new world of tomorrow by first of all annihilating the world of today."[13]

---

[12] Gilson, *The Terrors of the Year 2000*, 13–17.

[13] Gilson, *The Terrors of the Year 2000*, 17–18.

What, then, are we who oppose Nietzsche's project to do in the face of such a cataclysm? Nietzsche's plan, his mission, is to destroy "today to create tomorrow." Gilson considers forgivable that we should not have anticipated Nietzsche's advent. "But," he says, "that we should not understand what he is doing while he is doing it right under our eyes, just as we were told he would do it—that bears witness to a stranger blindness. Can it really be that the herd of human being that is led to the slaughter has eyes and yet does not see?" Gilson's explanation for such a depth of blindness is that announcement of a catastrophe of such an order usually leaves us "but a single escape: to disbelieve it and, in order not to believe, to refuse to understand."[14]

Those who reject the escape of sticking our heads in the sand while we are sheepishly led to the slaughterhouse have another choice: to recognize the reality of the enemy we face and the nature of his project and reasonably to oppose it. Postmodern man (actually modern man on steroids) is essentially Nietzschean. And his "mad ambition" is impossible to achieve. We choose the way we can, not the way we wish. We might wish to become absolutely free creators, creators *ex nihilo*, but, at best, our wish is an impossible dream.

True creation, Gilson rightly recognizes, is not fashioning material like a demiurge. It is a totally self-authoring gratuitous act, "the only act which is truly creative because it alone is truly free." As much as we might wish to become free in this strict sense, our *esse* is always *co-esse*, not *esse subsistens*. The nature of the material world confronts us, limits us, and determines the extent to which we can

[14] Gilson, *The Terrors of the Year 2000*, 17.

fashion and remodel it. "We shall perhaps be great manufacturers," Gilson tells us. "[B]ut creators—never. To create in his turn *ex nihilo*, man must first of all reestablish everywhere the void."[15]

This, then, has become postmodern man's project: mad ambition, everywhere to reestablish the void. On all sides, postmodern man feels Nietzsche's intoxicating joy, his mad delight, in the power of destruction. When Gilson says that Nietzsche is the Antichrist, he is speaking of Nietzsche metaphorically, much like Socrates says the Delphic oracle singled him out as an exemplar of wisdom in her cryptic message to his friend Chairephon that "no one is wiser than Socrates."[16] The Antichrist is postmodern man drunk "with the supremely lucid madness of a creature who would annihilate the obstacle which *being* places in the way of his creative ambitions. Such is the profound sense of our solemn and tragic adventure. Antichrist is not among us, he is in us. It is man himself, usurping unlimited creative power and proceeding to the certain annihilation of that which is, in order to clear the way for the problematic creation of all that will be."[17]

While Gilson does not say so specifically, the Antichrist as Gilson describes him as embodied in Nietzsche is the secularized ghost of Renaissance humanism haunting the Earth, the postmodern attempt *to supplant creation with metaphysical epic poetry effected through the unbridled free spirit of artistic destruction*. No wonder, then, that Gilson would turn to a critic of Stéphane Mallermé's poetic project to find just the right phraseology to describe "precisely

---

[15] Gilson, *The Terrors of the Year 2000*, 18–20.

[16] Plato, *Apology*, 23B.

[17] Gilson, *The Terrors of the Year 2000*, 20–21.

the sacrilegious effort whose meaning" he sought to unravel: "to construct a poetry which would have the value of preternatural creation and which would be able to enter into rivalry with the world of created things to the point of supplanting it totally."[18]

Postmodern man's project is universal surrealism, total release of human reason, of creative free spirit, from all metaphysical, moral, and aesthetic controls; the poetic spirit, the spirit of the artist gone totally mad with the intoxicating, surrealistic power of destruction. Once we destroy everything, nothing can stop us! Since the beginning of recorded time, God has gotten in the way of the artistic human spirit, has been the "eternal obstructor" to us being total self-creators. Now the tables are turned. With the advent of the post-modernity announced by Nietzsche, we have entered "the decisive moment of a cosmic drama."[19] Protagoras and Musaios have become Dionysus.

"Everything is possible," Gilson tells us, "provided only that this creative spark which surrealism seeks to disclose deep in our being be preceded by a devastating flame." Since "the massacre of values is necessary to create values that are really new," André Breton's description of "the most simple surrealist act" becomes perfectly intelligible and throws dramatic light upon the increasingly cavalier destruction of innocent life by terroristic acts of mass murder in our own day: "The most simple surrealist act consists in this: to go down into the streets, pistol in hand, and shoot at random for all you are worth, into the crowd."[20] (If we truly want to decrease incidences of

[18] Gilson, *The Terrors of the Year 2000*, 21–22.

[19] Gilson, *The Terrors of the Year 2000*, 20.

[20] Gilson, *The Terrors of the Year 2000*, 21–22.

contemporary mass murder and other acts of terrorism from the contemporary West [and the world], no one gives a better understanding of the nature of these phenomena and analysis of how to eradicate it than does Gilson.)

Since we human beings tend to be slow learners, Gilson notes that we have needed some time to grasp the full implications of the postmodern project. We have gotten out of the habit of talking about things like "divine law," but we still hold onto its vestige in our enlightened, secularized appeals to "the voice of conscience." Such appeals help us to pretend not to understand the catastrophic consequences of the grandiose sophistry of the postmodern project. If we pretend long enough that it does not exist, perhaps it will go away.

Unhappily, it will not. Gilson tells us that the father of postmodern man's existential project is Sisyphus, not Prometheus. Our destiny has become "the absurd" and "truly exhausting task" of perpetual self-invention without model, purpose, or rule. Having turned ourselves into gods, we do not know what to do with our divinity.[21]

But what will happen to us when more of us start to realize that the voice of conscience is the reflection of nothing, a convenient illusion we have created to maintain the intoxicating joy of our own poetic and sophistic project? Even drunkards, at times, tire of their alcoholism.

Gilson admonishes us that our postmodern story is really quite old. He recounts the story of Samuel from the *Book of Samuel* (8:7–22) in which the Jewish people, tired of being free, asked the aging prophet Samuel to make them a king to judge them, like all other nations had. While Samuel was saddened by their request and saw it

[21] Gilson, *The Terrors of the Year 2000*, 21–25.

as a rejection of him as a judge, God told him to grant the people's wish with the forewarning of the sorts of bondage that would beset them once their wish was fulfilled.[22]

Having freed ourselves from divine rule, the necessary political consequence for postmodern man is political enslavement by a totalitarian State. Having refused to serve God, we have no one left to judge the State, no arbiter between us and the State. Hence, Gilson tells us in 1948:

"In every land and in all countries, the people wait with fear and trembling for the powerful of this world to decide their lot for them. They hesitate, uncertain among the various forms of slavery which are being prepared for them. Listening with bated breath to the sounds of those countries which fall one after the other with a crash followed by a long silence, they wonder in anguish how long will last this little liberty they still possess. The waiting is so tense that many feel a vague consent to slavery secretly germinating within themselves. With growing impatience, they await the arrival of the master who will impose on them all forms of slavery starting with the most degrading of all—that of mind."[23]

Finding ourselves totally free to engage in the perpetual task of endless self-creation, Gilson tells us, we resemble a soldier on a twenty-four hour leave with nothing to do: totally bored in the tragic loneliness of an idle freedom we cannot productively use.[24] To Gilson's ears, the explosion of Hiroshima resounded a solemn metaphysical assertion of postmodern (better had he said "postmodern

---

[22] Gilson, *The Terrors of the Year 2000*, 26–27.

[23] Gilson, *The Terrors of the Year 2000*, 28.

[24] Gilson, *The Terrors of the Year 2000*, 24.

falsely-so-called") man's statement that, while we no longer want to be God's image, we can still be God's caricature. While we cannot create anything, we now possess the intoxicating power to destroy everything.

As a result, feeling totally empty and alone, postmodern man (actually "modern man on steroids) offers, to anyone willing to take it, the futile freedom he does not know how to use. "He is ready for all the dictators, leaders of these human herds who follow them as guides and who are all finally conducted by them to the same place—the *abbatoir*" (the slaughterhouse).[25]

So, then, now that Gilson's analysis of our 'postmodern' predicament has been told, what does he offer us in the way of a solution? Precisely the sort of advice we would expect from a true and serious philosopher. He admonishes us that we will not find the remedy for our predicament by wallowing in postmodernity's evil. We will find it by courageously seeking and attacking its *metaphysical* cause. "Let us not say: it is too late, and there is nothing left to do; but let us have the courage to look for the evil and the remedy where they exist."

Since "falsely-so-called" postmodernity's chief problem is that we have lost reason (*logos*) in touch with reality because we have lost God, Gilson tells us, our solution is simple. We will not find our reason and recover touch with reality again until we have "first found God again." And we will not find God again without the willingness "to receive what still remains of grace today."[26] To do that, we must turn our minds again to the world, to have them measured by the

---

[25] Gilson, *The Terrors of the Year 2000*, 28–29.

[26] Gilson, *The Terrors of the Year 2000*, 29.

being of things, not by our unbridled and unmoored poetic imaginations.

To Gilson, this means that we must attempt once again to inhabit the universe of St. Thomas in which the service of God and reason are compatible and produce in us order, beauty, and joy—not nausea—because, in this world, unlike the postmodern world, the necessary condition for the existence of one does not entail the necessary destruction of the other. For, sharing the same cause as part of the same creation, the order of our freedom, thoughts, and reality complement, they do not contradict, one another.

By submitting the measure of our minds to the being of things (which, as a practical matter, for Gilson, simultaneously entails implicit recognition of God's existence), Gilson thinks we have some hope of recovering our sanity and avoiding modernity's/postmodernity's slaughterhouse. He maintains that salvation for us today is the same as it was in Raoul Glaber's time. Glaber reported that, after all the impending anxiety, the fears of the year One Thousand subsided and peace came to the Earth. Only God can protect us from each other and ourselves. We "either serve Him in spirit and in truth," Gilson admonishes us, "or we shall enslave ourselves ceaselessly, more and more, to the monstrous idol which we have made with our own hands to our image and likeness."[27]

While what Gilson concludes in the *Terrors of the Year 2000* is true, it fails to add two things that crucially need to be said and Gilson has elsewhere maintained.

(1) As he tells us in the masterful *The Unity of Philosophical Experience*, since we are the bearers of Western culture, since it only

---

[27] Gilson, *The Terrors of the Year 2000*, 29–31.

exists in and through us and the cultural institutions we have caused, the West cannot be dying without our being aware of this reality.

By Western culture, broadly considered, Gilson says he essentially means the ancient Greek culture that the ancient Romans had inherited, which was subsequently transfused by the ancient Church Fathers with Christian religious teachings, and progressively increased by numerous artists, writers, philosophers, and scientists from the start of the Middle Ages to the present day.[28]

(2) Regarding this inherited cultural enterprise, Gilson asks a very sobering question: "Can a social order, begotten by a common faith in the value of certain principles, keep on living when all faith in these principles is lost?"

Best to illustrate the meaning of this question Gilson gives a summary description of two principles that, for him, constitute what, for brevity's sake, he calls "The Western Creed": two civilizational principles essential to the subsequent development of Western culture and all its cultural institutions.

Principle 1 is a firm belief of the ancient Greeks in the eminent dignity of human beings. As Gilson says:

> The Greeks of classical times never wavered in their conviction, that of all the things that can be found in nature, man is by far the highest, and that of all the things important for man to know, by far the most important is man. When Socrates, after unsuccessful attempts to deal with physical problems, made up his mind to dedicate himself to the exclusive

[28] Étienne Gilson, *The Unity of Philosophical Experience* (New York: Charles Scribner's Sons, 1963), 271–272.

> study of man, he was making a momentous decision. 'Know thyself' is not only the key to Greek culture, but to the classical culture of the Western world as well. What the Greeks left to their successors was a vast body of knowledge related to man's nature and his various needs: logic, which is the science of how to think; several different philosophies, all of them culminating in ethics and politics, which are the sciences of how to live; remarkable specimens of history and political eloquence, related to the life of the city. As to what today we call positive science, the greatest achievements of the Greek genius were along the lines of mathematics, a knowledge which man draws from his own mind without submitting to the degrading tyranny of material facts; and medicine, whose proper object is to ensure the well-being of the human body. And they stopped there, checked by an obscure feeling that the rest was not worth having, at least bit at the price which the human mind would have to pay for it: its freedom from matter, its internal liberty.[29]

Principle 2 is one that Gilson was convinced had culturally saved the ancient Greeks from constructing the monstrous idol which we in the modern and Enlightenment West have made with our own hands to modern and Enlightenment man's image and likeness. Hence, Gilson identifies the second essential principle of Western culture and the Western Creed that we had inherited from the an-

[29] Gilson, *The Unity of Philosophical* Experience, 272–273.

cient Greeks to be "the conviction that reason is the specific difference of human beings."[30] Try to transform man's specific difference from human reason and turn it into universal consciousness existing separated from the individual human body and Gilson maintains that we can no longer explain how a disembodied mind can regulate the human appetites and explain how human beings are moral agents. He states:

"Man is best described as a rational animal; deprive man of reason and what is left of man is not man, but animal. This looks like a very commonplace statement, yet Western culture is dying wherever it is forgotten: for the rational nature of man is the only foundation for a rational system of ethics. Morality is essentially normality; for a rational being to act either without reason or contrary to its dictates is to act and behave not exactly as a beast, but as a beastly man, which is worse. For it is proper that a beast should act as a beast, that is, according to its own nature; but it is totally unfitting for a man to act as a beast, because that means the total oblivion of his own nature, and hence his final destruction."[31]

Remarkable to Gilson is the centuries-long continuity within Western culture of these two principles inherited from the ancient Greeks by the subsequent generations. They had survived transmission to Christian culture, the Christian Middle Ages, renaissance humanism, the sixteenth-century Protestant Reformation, and even early modern discoveries in mathematical physics. So long as science remained faithful to its own philosophical, and chiefly metaphysical and moral, nature, Gilson says, "it remained the healthy exercise of

---

[30] Gilson, *The Unity of Philosophical Experience*, 274.

[31] Gilson, *The Unity of Philosophical Experience*, 274.

reason, reason seeking to know because knowing is its natural function."[32]

He adds that, "Even the most stupendous progress made by the physical and biological sciences entailed no disruption in the continuity of Western culture. While man remained in control of nature (that is, retained the self-understanding of being a rational, and chiefly metaphysical and moral animal), culture could survive. It was lost from the very moment nature began to control man (that is, from the moment science became transformed into the Nietzschean *will-to-power*)."[33]

Gradually, over several centuries, the dramatic material success of science re-conceived as productive and technical, mathematically-constrained knowledge essentially separated from metaphysics and ethics gradually causes Westerners "to despise all disciplines in which such demonstrations could not be found, or to rebuild those disciplines after the pattern of the physical sciences. As a consequence, metaphysics and ethics had to be either ignored or, at least, replaced by new positive sciences; in either case, they would be eliminated."[34]

Gilson considered this move to be very dangerous, one that explains "perilous position in which Western culture has now found itself. The European burnt of his old ships before making sure that the new ones would float. Moreover, the first article of the scientific creed is the acceptance of nature as it is. Far from making up for the

[32] Gilson, *The Unity of Philosophical* Experience, 275–276.

[33] Gilson, *The Unity of Philosophical* Experience, 276. My comments added in parentheses.

[34] Gilson, *The Unity of Philosophical* Experience, 276.

loss of philosophy, the discovery of scientific substitutes for it leaves man alone with nature such as it is and obliges him to surrender to natural necessity.

Philosophy is the only rational knowledge by which both science and nature can be judged. By reducing philosophy to pure science (that is, the productive contemporary activity of mathematical physics), man had not only abdicated his right to judge nature and to rule it; but he has also turned himself into a particular aspect of nature, subjected like all the rest, to the necessary law which regulates its development. A world where accomplished facts are their own justification is ripe for the most reckless social adventures. Its dictators can wantonly play havoc with human institutions and human lives, for dictatorships are facts and they also are unto themselves their own justifications.[35]

Gilson was convinced that, if we in the West lose philosophy as the ancient Greeks had conceived it, we will lose commitment to the Western Creed. In so doing, he cautioned, "we are bound to lose Western culture itself together with the feeling for the eminent dignity of man." The future of the West as he saw it was one of "an aimlessly drifting wreck, or a ship holding a steady course with a rational animal at the wheel."[36]

Clearly, Gilson thought that, in having replaced the Western Creed with the Enlightenment Scientific Creed, the contemporary West had introduced into our culture a form of psychosis that looks to irrationality as the last bulwark of liberty against a dictatorship of

---

[35] Gilson, *The Unity of Philosophical Experience* 277.

[36] Gilson, *The Unity of Philosophical Experience*, 295. My addition in the parenthesis within the paragraph.

scientific reason and the technological system of control that it tends to generate into all our contemporary cultural institutions (like colleges and universities, political parties, religious organizations, and intellectual societies). Such being the case, and since, as Gilson tells us, (1) we are the bearers of Western culture; (2) Western culture only exists in and through us and the cultural institutions we have caused; and (3) simply as discrete individuals and disparate multitudes, we cannot recover the West dying within us. *We can only do so as essential psychological parts, team-members, of a culture we are aware is dying within us and our cultural institutions.*

The ancient Greeks had not developed philosophy through the work of disconnected individuals, or within a short span of time. They had done so as part of a culturally-conscious, psychological enterprise, cultural team effort, to escape from the slavery they had recognized always accompanies the barbarism that human irrationality tends to generate. They had inherited their sense of philosophical wonder and conviction about the eminent dignity of the human person as a rational animal through centuries of habituation in a cultural, transgenerational psychology (or public philosophy) chiefly generated out of moral and metaphysical principles transmitted through centuries of work of ancient Greek artists, poets, somewhat sound religious and political leaders, and the teachings of a Socratic public philosophy of uncommon sense (Socratic organizational psychology) born out of, and exercised within, the Agora in Athens.

We can expect nothing different today. As Jacques Maritain, Mortimer J. Adler, and Étienne Gilson had recognized decades ago, to retrieve philosophy in our cultural institutions, we will first have to do yeoman's work of recovering it through a public philosophy within a renewed cultural psychology transmitted initially through the common and uncommon common sense of the general population in everyday activities. Time is getting late. Please join us in this effort, with the help of grace, to turn our souls again to the world, to have them measured by the being of things, God, and a reason in touch with reality, and not by our unbridled and unmoored poetic imaginations and the despotism and terrorism it tends to generate.

Chapter 6

Gilson, Europe, and The New World Order

When, in Lesson 1 of his *Commentary on the Metaphysics of Aristotle*, St. Thomas Aquinas begins his report of how Aristotle had started talking about the history of the origin of the concept of philosophy, science, among the Ancient Greeks and other Mediterranean cultures prior to them, he had described this as an individual and community team enterprise: a 'prudent,' organizational act of an organizational whole. The people involved in starting this organization shared a common, *prudent*, chief aim: to escape from the damaging effects they had commonly recognized brute-animal ignorance causes.[1]

They could not have proceeded in this way had they not shared a common concept and understanding: 1) of human beings as a unique species of animal: 'a rational animal;' and 2 of Aristotle's admonition in his book '*On the Heavens* (*de Caelo*) that small mistakes in the start of an investigation tend to "multiply a thousandfold as the investigation proceeds."[2] In addition, to talk somewhat like a student of Georg Hegel (b.1770; d.1831), they had thought of themselves as conceiving of philosophy, science, as 'a world-historical concept.'

---

[1] St. Thomas Aquinas, *Commentary on the Metaphysics of Aristotle*, Bk. 1, lect. 1; see, especially, n. 11.

[2] Aristotle, *De Caelo*, Bk. 1. 1, Ch. 5, A271.

'Strictly speaking,' they had not conceived of themselves as: (1) an organizational community engaged in some sort of cultural revolution; (2) Europeans; or (3) Westerners. They could not have done so because, 'strictly speaking,' none of these concepts had precisely existed during their time.

When philosophy had first started to arise among ancient Greeks colonists in Asia-Minor (near modern-day Turkey, in Miletus and Ionia) around the 7th and 6th centuries, B.C., the Ancient Greeks had conceived of the world as they knew it to consist in lands surrounding the Aegean Sea. This became the later-known 'Mediterranean' ('Middle Land') geographical region: 'the Middle of the Roman Empire' as the Romans later conceived of it.

To the peoples living in the lands surrounding the Aegean Sea during the time of the start of Ancient Greek philosophy, the concept of 'the World' consisted of: (1) 'lands to the East' (Asia); (2) 'lands to the South' (Libya); and (3) 'lands to the West and North' (the geographical region that later became called 'Europe').

Etymologically, the word 'Europe' is derived from *Europa*—the name of a Phoenician (modern Lebanon) princess who was the mother of King Minos of Crete, whom the god Zeus had abducted as a wife. In addition, the Ancient Greeks had referred to 'Euros' as their northernmost province of Thrace and to the river that flowed through it. Before the term 'Europe' became used to refer to a continent (around the ninth century, A.D.), it was often used to refer to Thrace.

During the ninth-century Carolingian Renaissance, the term 'Europe' started to designate 'the area of cultural and political influence and continent' controlled in the 'Western Roman Empire' by the Roman Catholic Church (the modern West) as distinct from 'the areas of political and cultural influence and geographical regions of the 'Eastern Roman Empire,' mainly influenced by Eastern Orthodox Catholic Churches and Islam.

I mention this short history of the beginnings of the philosophical and cultural concept of 'Europe' in the West prior to the start and end of World War II because, just after the end ot World War II, like many intellectuals and politicians at the time, Étienne Gilson had become increasingly interested in: 1) understanding the idea and nature of 'Europe' and 2) developing a *New World Order*, that would: 1) never again allow world wars to happen; and 2) issue in a new political world order that would create lasting peace. As a student of Aristotle and St. Thomas Aquinas, Gilson well knew that, at the start of any investigation he had to be careful precisely to understand the first principles of his investigations. In his present research, one such principle was the precise philosophical, historical, origin and definition of the concept and nature of 'Europe'!

In part, his reason for undertaking this investigation was that, as World War II came to an end, Gilson had started to become increasingly devoted to realizing the possibility of that *ordre catholique* he had advocated in the 1930s. He was convinced that German Hitlerism, Russian Communism, Italian and Spanish Fascism and American Deweyism had stood in the way of realizing this *ordre* because each of them had focused on the production of their own brand of citizen, and not of them had seen a pressing need for the teaching of moral and intellectual virtue. Nonetheless, at this time he had thought real changes were finally possible. None had understood the need for starting their investigation with a proper understanding of the nature of the subject they were proposing to investigate.

In 1945, to start to address these problems, Gilson wrote an article for *Le monde* entitled "Instruire ou éduquer?"in which he argued for the need to: (1) have greater concern for students as individuals, not prospective adherents to a political cause, and (2) familiarize students from infancy with moral virtues of the individual such as honor, duty, justice, and piety. Having reat St. Thomas Aquinas Summa contra gentiles, Gilson realize that, as a wise man he had a duty (*officium*, in Latin: a moral office) to seek to understand the whole truth about the nature of his subject and to refute opposing errors to that truth.[3]

He quickly followed this article with four others that had the same keynote theme: "The first step of any totalitarian regime is to seize the schools in order to have exclusive monopoly over shaping tomorrow's citizens." *In these articles, Gilson sought to focus educators' attention on inculcating personal virtue*, not the power of political movements. He entitled them: (1) "Hitler fera-t-il notre revolution?"; (2) "La circulaire 45 ou: comment l'on se propose de pervertir la vérité"; (3) "La revolution ou l'amitié redressera la Cite"; and (4) "La schisme national." He published the articles in Stanislas Fumet's religiously-oriented journal *Hebdomadaire du temps present*.

About a month after publishing these articles, Gilson published "Pour une education nationale" in *La vie intelletuelle*. Therein, *he argued that free education must include religion*. Apparently, before

[3] St. Thomas Aquinas, *Summa contra gentiles*, Bk. 2, Ch. 1.

going to print, the Journal's editor sent the article to General Charles de Gaulle, who read it shortly thereafter. In another article published around this same time in *La croix*, entitled "La liberté de l'enseignement en Angleterre," Gilson expressed his admiration for the open British conformist and non-conformist educational policy in contrast to France's closed State-controlled one.

On 15 March 1945, Gilson spoke before a packed meeting of "La Jeunesse Intellectuelle" in La Grande Salle de la Mutualité. As a result of these educational works, Gilson started to correspond with many of the leading intellectuals in post-liberation France and to become recognized as a spokesman for them. As a result, the French Ministry of Foreign Affairs selected him to join his friend Jacques Maritain as part of the French delegation the 1945 San Francisco meeting to plan the United Nations charter, which was signed on 26 June of that year.

After returning to Toronto for a few months in anticipation of teaching his fall courses there, the French Foreign Ministry informed him that the Ministry had named him to participate in the October and November 1945 London conference designed to create the constitution for what would later become UNESCO, the United Nations Educational, Scientific, and Cultural Organization. Gilson served on the committee that drafted UNESCO's constitution.

During his stay in London, Gilson wrote five articles about the conference that were published in *Le monde*. Several others appeared over the next several years. In them, among other things, Gilson expressed his disappointment about the limited roles intellectuals would actually have in UNESCO. He also later expressed disappointment about the behavior of intellectuals at

UNESCO's first general conference in Paris in 1946. In a radio discussion in which he took part with several other conference participants after the meeting regarding the question "Can UNESCO Educate for World Understanding?," *Gilson maintained that the world would not be ready for global understanding until university education became more international than it then was.*

In April 1946, Gilson went to Rome to participate in meetings of the Pontifical Academy of Thomas Aquinas and an international meeting to establish *Pax Romana* as an international movement of intellectuals engaged in the service of God. At the Pontifical Academy he spoke on "The Knowledge of Being." At *Pax Romana* he talked about "Les intellectuals dans la chrétienté" (published in the same year in *Travaux et documents*).

While Gilson was engaged in these intellectual activities, he had also become involved in the anti-communist *Mouvement Républicaine Populaire* (MRP). Thinking that, as a politician, at the time he might be able to influence educational reform, Gilson accepted a two-year appointment as a senator on the *Conseil de la République.* Partly as a result of these new political activities, Paul Martin, Minister of Health and Welfare in Mackenzie King's Liberal government, invited Gilson to address a Young Liberals Conference at McMaster University, Hamilton, Ontario on the subject of democracy scheduled for the first week of September 1947. Gilson later repeated the talk, which he had entitled "The Philosophy of Liberalism," to the Political Science Club at the University of Toronto. The journal *Canada Looks Ahead* later published the address under the title "The Task of the Democratic State."

In the talk, among other things, Gilson argued for the need for the modern state to condemn oppression of individual freedom and extend and guarantee personal freedom, including economic and social freedom, and personal property ownership, to everyone.

Early in May 1948, Gilson participated in a meeting of the *Congress of United Europe* in The Hague to discuss plans for a united Europe. He then published an article about the meeting in the paper *Une semaine dans le monde* and in an unpublished typescript that he wrote in 1950 entitled "Existe-t-il une culture éuropéenne?" On 10 May 1948, he spoke at the Cité-Club in Paris of the need for religious freedom in education as essential to the existence of intellectual freedom. From 13 August to 18 September 1948, Gilson published several articles in *Le monde* expressing his disappointment with professional politics. In December 1948, Gilson's professional political career ended with his realization "that there is no difference between being a senator and being nothing."

Shortly after Gilson returned to Canada in September 1949, he delivered an evening lecture at St. Thomas More College of Saskatoon on "St. Thomas More and the Law." He followed this with a lecture the next morning at the University of Saskatchewan on "Politics and Philosophy." In the article, Gilson argued about the relationship among tolerance, dogmatism, skepticism, and truth. He maintained that no necessary connection exists between dogmatism and intolerance or skepticism and tolerance.

He claimed that skeptics qua skeptics cannot be tolerant and dogmatists qua dogmatists need not be intolerant. Skeptics qua skeptics can only be permissive, not tolerant. Strictly speaking, only the person who admits the existence of truth can be tolerant. Gilson argued further that tolerance is a moral, not an intellectual, virtue rooted in the political virtues of justice and friendship; and that tolerance and intolerance exist essentially in the political, not the intellectual, order. This lecture was subsequently published in the University's journal *Le Sheaf.* Gilson expanded the lecture, presented it at Rutgers University, and later published it under the title "Dogmatism and Tolerance."

Early in January, 1950, Gilson presented a currently unpublished address to the MRP in Paris about "Political Liberty and the Parties." In the talk Gilson praised the movement's respect for the individual freedom of its deputies to be able to think for themselves, not tow the party line. He claimed that the Party's program: (1) regarded the family, not the political party, as the real center of French social organization; (2) would not nationalize industry unless needed for normal production and distribution; (3) would support revolutionary union objectives only if they were legitimate; (4) would treat every French citizen as an individual moral agent possessed of intellect, will, and the faculty of free choice—not as a number; and (5) advocated no State religion, official science or philosophy, and did not discriminate in the area of teaching.

At this time Gilson regularly wrote political articles for *Le monde.* In one, "1940 to 1950," he described monarchists as "historical paleontologists" and accused Charles Maurras of being a "collaborator." He was, also, regularly critical of claims made by US politicians because, apparently, he thought that American foreign policy was largely based upon self-interest and that European politicians who reached out for US support also tended to do so out of self-interest. He thought that France's best interest at the time lay in neutrality between the Russia and the USA. He wrote three articles in *Le Monde* advocating European neutrality in case of war between the US and Russia: (1) "Défaitisme et neutralité," (2) "La neutralité vers l'est," and (3) "La neutralité vers l'ouest." At the time, to Gilson's amazement, some people accused him of being a "crypto-Communist" and "anti-American."

Continuing his political work as a trained philosopher and historian seeking a better understanding of the concept and nature of Europe and Christianity, in March 1950, Gilson went to Sweden, where, between 12 March and 02 April, he delivered eight lectures on St. Augustine.

At an after-dinner party the evening he delivered this last talk, Shook reports that Gilson happened to speak about the dangers he thought "an unarmed, partisan France faced from Russia." On Sunday, 03 December, Gilson repeated at Marquette the fourth lecture he had given at Notre Dame. After returning to Toronto on Monday, 04 December, on 12 December, Gilson wrote the French Ministry of Public Instruction that he wanted to retire from his position at the Collège de France starting 01 January 1951, something that he was legally entitled to do. He had wanted to divide his time almost equally between France and North America and to devote the next three years to teaching at the Toronto Institute to which he had given birth and had started to see grow.

After 1951 until 1957, when Canadian income tax laws became too prohibitive for Gilson to work there, Gilson would spend seven months in Canada and five in France. After that, until he left Canada entirely, he would spend three months in Canada and the rest in France. 1952 was a busy year for Gilson during which he lectured extensively on three main themes: (1) ethics and education, (2) contemporary science and philosophy, and (3) Christendom as the City of God.

He gave his first talk on 02 February, Candlemas Day, to St. Michael's College Adult Education Program on "The Breakdown of Morals and Christian Education." He later repeated this talk, which was published twice, at St. John Fisher College, Rochester, New York, and other places.

On 22 February, he spoke before the Alliance Française in Toronto. Between 27 and 31 March, he gave three talks at the University of Montreal and one for the Institut Franco-Canadien (also in Montreal). In mid-April, he read a paper on "Science, Philosophy, and Religious Wisdom" at the annual meeting of the American Catholic Philosophical Association (ACPA), published the same year in the Association's *Proceedings*, on the occasion of receiving the Association's *Cardinal Spellman Aquinas Medal.* Also in April, he delivered a radio version of this paper entitled "Religious Wisdom and Scientific Knowledge."

On 23 April, Gilson flew to Belgium to: (1) give a series of ten lectures between 29 April and 19 May on changing understandings of the City of God and (2) dedicate the Cardinal Mercier Chair at the University of Louvain. Those lectures served as the proximate first principles of Gilson's monograph, *Metamorphoses of the City of God* and the first attempts after World War II to form a European Union.

Since Gilson had given ten lectures given at the Louvain served as the basis for Gilson's *Metamorphoses of the City of God*, no wonder should exist why Gilson divided this monograph into ten

Chapter, which he named as follows: One: "Origin of the Problem"; Two: "The City of God"; Three: "The Christian Commonwealth: Four: "The Universal Empire"; Five: "On the Peace of Faith"; Six: "The City of the Sun; Seven: "The Birth of Europe"; Eight: "The City of the Philosophers; Nine: "The City of Scientists"; and Ten: "The Church and Universal Society."

Considered as a whole, like Augustine's *City of God*, the monograph is a rhetorical work (a work in apologetics) that Gilson's *officium*, like Augustine's, morally obliged him to produce. Its chief aim is to consider the nature, and proper concept, of a city (*civitas*) as Augustine had defined it as "a people"; and "a people" as "a multitude of rational beings joined together by common agreement on the objects of their love."[4]

In so doing mainly as a historian, Gilson sees Augustine's 'city'to be the 'City of God' precisely because its birth coincided with the birth of Christendom. For Augustine, the City of God is a Heavenly City—one that can never be fully realized on Earth. In fact, any attempt to establish this city of Earth can only produce a flawed caricature of it that is doomed from the start to fail. Its first principles do not allow it to succeed.

Just as the first of the ancient Western philosophers had conceived of Europe as the World as they knew it—the cultural milieu and situation in which they found themselves to exist, where planetary unity as they knew it existed within the midst of "travails," "weaknesses," and "convulsions" of which Gilson said "we are the

[4] St. Aurelius Augustine, *de Civitate Dei*, XIX.24. Note that my analysis of Gilson's *Metamorphoses of the City of God*, is based, in part, on my reading of James G. Colbert's beautiful English translation of this work.

causes or victims." Local history did not exist; and, strictly speaking, it has never existed. Gilson glaringly points out this reality in Chapter One of his monograph in relation to the condition of the modern city he found himself inhabiting in 1952. About it he says:

> What characterizes the events we witnesss, what distinguishes them from everything that preceded them since the beginnings of history is their world character, as they say, or planetary character, as perhaps it might be more aptly put. There is no longer local history. There is no longer exclusively national history whose events concern a particular people and it alone, in the sense that this people alone os the cause or will undergo the effects of those events. Planetary unity has been achieved. Economic, industrial, and technical reasons in general, all of which we can view as *de facto* solidarity among peoples of the earth. Consequently, their vicissitudes are combined in a universal history of which they are the particular aspects. Whatever the difference of peoples of the world may think about it, they have become parts of a humanity that is more natural than social. Henceforth, they must become aware of that humanity in order to will it, instead of just undergoing it, and in order to think about it with a view to organizing it.[5]

Most remarkable to me about what Gilson says in the above passage is how mistaken he appears to be in pretty much all the

[5] Gilson, *Metamorphoses of the City of God*, 3–4.

claims he makes within it. While, the U.S Speaker of the House for ten years, Tip O'Neil might have been right when he said that, for a politician, "All politics is local," for all human beings, for all times and places, politics is always more than local, is always planetary. And since the birth of nation states, it has always been international.

However, when we consider this passage within the context of: 1) Gilson's 1948, St. Michael's College opuscule *The Terrors of the Year 2000*, and 2) his statement in the above passage that the term "planetary character" might be a more apt term to use to describe the "travails," "weaknesses," and "convulsions" that he and other Westerners had undergone during the time of World War II and its aftermath, all Gilson's claims appear to be 'spot on,' not 'mistaken.' After World War II, Western intellectuals started increasingly to think about human beings as more than geographically and parts of the world. They began increasingly to consider us to be *planetary.*[6]

One reason this shift intellectual thinking had started to occur was because, while prior to World War II, they had recognized that all human beings had been geographically parts of planet Earth as parts of a geographical region that was qualitatively bigger and stronger than they were: *Mother Nature*. After World War II, however, for the first time in human history, human beings had become 'planetary' in an entirely new way. We had acquired the ability entirely to destroy planet Earth! We had now become qualitatively bigger and stronger than planet Earth and Mother Nature.

---

[6] See, for example, existentialist philosopher Wilfrid Desan's book *The Planetary Man* (New York and United Kingdom, 1962).

Prior to World War II, world wars had always been somewhat geographically limited. Cities and States that controlled naval power and had advanced weaponry for the time tended to dominate world conflicts and planet Earth in their geographical regions. Hence, Athens and Sparta, the ancient Roman, Persian, and Egyptian Empires dominated world wars in the West. Empires like Rome could take advantage of their geographical location protected by the Alps and Mediterranean Sea, at least until Hannibal was able to cross the Alps with his elephants. African regions could take advantage of vast stretches of desert. But Hannibal was no match for *The Desert Fox*, Erwin Rommel and his tanks. In the Far East, China could depend upon its 'Great Wall' to protect it from invaders. And Roman Emperor Hadrian was able to build his famous 'Wall" in Britain to secure Roman domination of it for over three centuries.

Nevertheless, for the first time in human history, invention of the airplane changed the nature of modern warfare to become truly planetarily global. Being a 'Mistress of the Seas' no longer guaranteed military dominance. Nor did being a geographically big country with a large population and lots of physical resources.

During World War II, German use of V-2 (*Vergeltungswaffen*-2, in German) bombs made missiles more powerful than airplanes as weapons. And, as many intellectuals like Gilson had realized at the time, the invention of the Atomic Bomb during World War II and the Hydorgen Bomb after it made modern warfare something no longer tolerable for the the future existence of humanity on planet Earth. Hence, Gilson's rush as a historian and a man conscious of having a professional *officium* (moral responsibility) after World War II, to help eradicate this problem.

As he said in Chapter One of his *Metamorphoses of the City of God*, the historian has a role to play in organizing, not "just undergoing," the new world order developing around us. Hence, analogously spot on was Gilson's claim: "Whatever the difference of peoples of the world may think about it, they have become parts of a humanity that is more natural than social. Henceforth, they must become aware of that humanity in order to will it, instead of just undergoing it, and in order to think about it with a view to organizing it."[7]

Upon first reading it, a person might be inclined to consider Gilson's above claim to be ridiculous. How can peoples of the world become "parts of a humanity that is more natural than social"? By nature, all human beings are social animals. We can never become more natural than social.

I suspect Gilson's response would have been, "By becoming, by nature, more 'animal' than 'rational'—by becoming Nietzschean and by having transformed ourselves into God and human science into a psychological habit that: 1) no longer seeks to study physical nature so as to understand it, but now seeks to study it to destroy it. I say I suspect this would have benn Gilson's response because, when I first read this passage, I could not help myself, harkening back to these frightening words Gilson had uttered in *Terrors of the Year 2000*, which I had mentioned in Chapter Five of this monograph:

Gilson then referred to the devastation of World War I, millions of dead, his own vision of children's corpses in Ukranian villages

---

[7] Gilson, *Metamorphoses of the City of God*, 3–4.

and on the banks of the Volga; wandering "bands of children reduced to savagery," later mowed down with machine guns; and official documentation bearing witness to the fact that "parents devoured their children. Fathers and mothers like our own, like ourselves, but who knew the meaning of that frightful word: 'hunger.'"[8]

Communism overtook Holy Russia and threatened the whole world. An armistice, misnamed 'peace,' followed from 1918 until World War II. During this time, China remained in a comstate state of war, while a "barbarous civil war" followed in "Most Christian Spain."

During 1930s, for a second time, "the German army hurled itself upon Europe for a second time, vanquishing, plundering, butchering Poland, toppling Paris, and astonishing the world." Air bombardments filled the skies of France, the South Sea Islands, China, Russia, Germany, Italy, and England and destroyed Britains once great navy.

"The atomic bombing of Hiroshima followed the genocidal holocaust against the Jews and led to a contemporary age in which the close of World War II yielded no lasting peace and gave birth to the dawn of a new era "where science, formerly our hope and our joy, would be the source of greatest terror."[9]

At the close of World War II, in short, Gilson saw human beings making our most astounding discovery, whose symbolism he found more striking because it was involuntary: "the great secret that science has just wrested from matter is the secret of its destruction. To know today is synonymous with to destroy."

---

[8] Gilson, *The Terrors of the Year 2000*, 5–7.

[9] Gilson, *The Terrors of the Year 2000*, 7.

Gilson asserted that human discovery of nuclear fission consisted an inseparable union of good and evil involving: 1) "the most intimate revelation of the nature of the physical world"; 2) "the freeing of the most powerful energy that has ever been held"; and 3) "the most frightful agent of destruction which man has ever had at his disposal." He said, "The age of atomic physics will see the birth of a new world, as different from our own age as ours is from the world before steam and electricity." This new world presents the scientist with a tragic dilemma. We know so many things today that our science might preclude our ability to control our own domination. In former times, Gilson says, we human beings mastered nature by obeying her. From now on, he claims, we master nature by destroying her.[10]

Atomic physics is only the beginning. Succeeding the era of physics, Gilson predicts we will witness "the still more redoubtable one of biology." He says that very few laboratory workers of his day doubt "we are on the verge of a great mystery which may, any day, surrender its secret. We will be able to work, not only on inert matter, but even on life, and it is not only the breadth of our power but its very nature which will become terrifying; and the more so that here again, and for the same reason, the possibility of good is inseparable from that of evil."[11]

He predicted:

"The biology of tomorrow will allow more subtle, but not the less formidable, interventions in human destiny. Can we imagine the repercussions which the free determinations of the sexes will have

---

[10] Gilson, *The Terrors of the Year 2000*, 7–9.

[11] Gilson, *The Terrors of the Year 2000*, 9.

some day, perhaps in the near future? Can we picture what would happen in a world where we could not only turn out males and females at will, but select them and produce human beings adapted to various functions as do breeders with dogs or horses or cattle? In that future society which will know how to give itself slaves and even the reproducers which it needs, what will become of the liberty and dignity of the human person? For once, the most daring prophecies of H. G. Wells appear tame, for in *The Island of Dr. Moreau* they were still only working to transform wild brutes into men; in the future society, it is men whom they will be transforming into brutes—to use them to foster the ends of a humanity thenceforth unworthy of the name."[12]

Gilson considered Nietzsche's declaration of the *Death of God* to be, "the capital discovery of modern times." Compared to Nietzsche's discovery, Gilson maintained that, no matter how far back we trace human history, we "will find no upheaval to compare with this in the extent or in the depth of its cause." To Gilson Nietzsche's declaration of God's death signaled a metaphysical revolution of the highest, widest, and deepest order.

Clearly by the end of World War II Gilson had recognized the terrors to follow would be in root cause, metaphysical. The chief clash of civilizations the world would face would not between the politics of West and East, or the West and other political orders. It would be a metaphysical clash between the ancient and modern West.

---

[12] Gilson, *The Terrors of the Year 20009*, 9–11.

Gilson maintained that, from time immemorial, we in the West had based our cultural creed and scientific inspiration upon a common conviction that we inhabited a providential order in which that gods, or a God, existed. All of our Western intellectual and cultural institutions had presupposed the existence of a God or gods. After Nietzsche, this was no longer true. All of a sudden, "God no longer exists. Worse: He never existed! The implication is clear: We shall have to change completely our every thought, word and deed. The entire human order totters on its base."

While, to my knowledge, Gilson never sais so specifically, the Antichrist as Gilson described him as embodied in Nietzsche is the secularized ghost of Renaissance humanism haunting the Earth, the postmodern attempt *to supplant creation with metaphysical epic poetry effected through the unbridled free spirit of artistic destruction.* No wonder exists for me, then, that Gilson would turn to a critic of Stéphane Mallermé's poetic project to find just the right phraseology to describe Nietzsche's grandiose project for what it precisely is, a sacrilegious effort meant to construct a poetry that "would have the value of preternatural creation and which would be able to enter into rivalry with the world of created things to the point of supplanting it totally."[13]

Gilson saw postmodern man's project as a "universal surrealism, total release of human reason, of creative free spirit, from all metaphysical, moral, and aesthetic controls; the poetic spirit, the spirit of the artist gone totally mad with the intoxicating, surrealistic power

[13] Gilson, *The Terrors of the Year 2000*, 21–22.

of destruction. Once we destroy everything, postmodern man thinks nothing can stop us!

"Everything is possible," Gilson tells us, "provided only that this creative spark which surrealism seeks to disclose deep in our being be preceded by a devastating flame." Since "the massacre of values is necessary to create values that are really new," André Breton's description of "the most simple surrealist act" becomes perfectly intelligible and throws dramatic light upon the increasingly cavalier destruction of innocent life by terroristic acts of mass murder in our own day: "The most simple surrealist act consists in this: to go down into the streets, pistol in hand, and shoot at random for all you are worth, into the crowd."[14] (If we truly want to decrease incidences of contemporary mass murder and other acts of terrorism from the contemporary West [and the world], no one gives a better understanding of the nature of these phenomena and analysis of how to eradicate it than does Gilson.)

To Gilson's ears, the explosion of Hiroshima resounded a solemn metaphysical assertion of postmodern (better had he said "postmodern falsely-so-called") man's statement that, while we no longer want to be God's image, we can still be God's caricature. While we cannot create anything, we now possess the intoxicating power to destroy everything.

Since "falsely-so-called" postmodernity's chief problem is that, having lost God, we have lost reason (*logos*) in touch with reality, and with it, common sense, Gilson tells us, our solution is simple.

---

[14] Gilson, *The Terrors of the Year 2000*, 21–22.

We will not find our reason and recover touch with reality again until first constructed a new world order in which we could find God again. And Gilson realized tht we could not not find God again without the willingness "to receive what still remains of grace today."[15] To do that, we would have to our minds again to the world and have them measured by the being of things—not by our unbridled and unmoored poetic imaginations. This is precisely what Gilson sought to do in writing his *Metamorphoses of the City of God.*

As a historian, Gilson thought he had a role to play in resolving this terrifying contemporary problem of organizing the 'New World Order" because, as a historian, his job is to reflect upon the data of the problem. As he said, "There is hardly any problem that will not be clarified by reflection upon its data."[16] As a real philosopher and man of uncommon common sense, Gilson knew that this job (*officium*) required wisdom, prudence—the tools used by a real philosopher.

Using the tools of both a real historian and real philosopher, before considering what Augustine says about the nature of the City of God in Chapter Two, in Chapter One, he first asks what the Romans had first considered a city to be. His answer was that a city was "a people united by common *descent*" from the same families and the same race religious practices.[17] According to Gilson, "Founded on the religious cult of the hearth, that is, upon the real domestic fire and not a mere metaphor, each family consisted of a closed society. It was separated from others by its own cult" with its own gods, own

[15] Gilson, *The Terrors of the Year 2000*, 29.

[16] Gilson, *The Terrors of the Year* 2000, 4.

[17] Gilson, *Metamorphoses of the City of God*, 3–4.

sets of common prayers, and forms of worship.[18] In short, in ancient Rome, religion (cult), not leisure nor anything else, was the basis, proximate first principle and cause, of culture. Leisure, culture, was not, and never has been, the basis of cities, culture, and civilizations!

Especially striking to me about Gilson making note of how the ancient Romans had understood *common descent from historical ancestors* to be the 'genus' that generated their idea and understanding of a city is that this understanding of a 'genus' is the first of four senses of a "genus" that St. Thomas Aquinas cites in his *Commentary of the Metaphysics of Aristotle.*[19] This first, or *historical* sense, differs from the sense in which: 1) logicians tend to understand a 'genus': as the chief subject of a common definition; 2) philosophers, scientists, consider it loosely as the subject that contains within it the proximate causes of the activity of a real genus; and 3) how these same philosophes, scientists consider it as the formal object of their distinctive habit of philosophy, science.

As a historian, Gilson is mainly interested in Augustine's understanding of a 'genus' in the first sense. As a philosopher, social scientist, he is chiefly interested in Augustine's understanding of a 'genus' in the fourth sense. In the first sense, a 'genus' is some organization whole that contains within it the formal cause, or essential nature, that generates its organizational activity. In the second sense, a 'genus,' is that formal cause, essential nature, abstractly considered as a common definition of all the subject of which it is properly pred-

---

[18] Gilson, *Metamorphoses of the City of God*, 4–5.

[19] *Commentary on the Metaphysics of Aristotle*, Bk. 5, lect. 22, nn. 1121–1144; Bk. 10, lect. 12, nn. 2142–2144.

icated. In the third sense, a 'genus' is that same formal cause, or essential nature, considered as existing within some subject that generates its organizational action. In the fourth sense, a 'genus' is the formal object of situational interest that is that is moving the habit of a philosopher, scientist to exercise his or her habit in some situation in the here and now. This is the sense of a 'genus' in which Étienne Gilson, the historian and philosopher starts to exercise his job (*officium*) in Chapter Two of the *Metamorphoses of the City of God.* Therein, he talks about how Augustine chiefly reflects upon a city properly understood as a "a multitude of rational beings joined together by common agreement on the objects of their love." According to Augustine, such a city must be founded upon justice. As Augustine said in his *City of God*, "Justice being taken away, then, what are kingdoms but great robberies?"[20]

According to Gilson, Augustine goes so far as to maintain, in agreement with tbe definition given by Marcus Tullius Cicero of a 'real society,' that when Rome had lost all justice at some moment in its history, it ceased to existed as a real society. Worse than this, Augustine says, according to Cicero's definition of a real society as one engendered by true justice, Rome never existed as a real society. It existed as a caricature of one. According to Augustine the only city that can be a real city is one in which Christ is the ruler.

Nonetheless, given the evident fact that moral virtues had existed in ancient Rome and that, to some extent, Rome had existed as a *res publica*, a "*people's thing*, an organization engendered by the virtues of its people, according to Gilson, Augustine finally relented

[20] St. Aurelius Augustine, *City of God*, Bk. IV.

and revised his definition of a people and a city as "a multitude of rational beings joined together by common agreement on the objects of their love."[21]

As a result of this distinction, Augustine's *City of God* becomes the story about two cities, two societies, distinguished by the chief objects of their love. According to Gilson, "This summary of the history of the two loves…contains the summary of universal history" (containing Gilson's in his *Metamorphoses of the City of God,* I need to add) including the ultimate root of all its intelligibility. Tell me what a people loves, and I will tell you what it is.

This is precisely what Gilson subsequently does in his *Metamorphoses of the City of God,* in which he starts to describe the de-divinization, increasing secularization, and final destruction of Augustine's City of God and all future cities and human societies from Sir Francis Bacon to the self-declared *Anti-Christ,* Friedrich Nietzsche.

Amen.

---

[21] Gilson, *Metamorphoses of the City of God*, 36–37.

Made in the USA
Middletown, DE
10 November 2024